A Lakeland Climbing Pioneer

John Wilson Robinson
of Whinfell Hall

Michael Waller

Bookcase

Full-length portrait of JWR

Acknowledgments

There are a number of people without whose help this book could not have been written. In particular I am indebted to Bev Rowland, whose exceptional familiarity with the world of climbing and extensive library on it have been so generously put at my disposal. Invaluable, too, has been the help of Polly Jones, the great-grand-niece of John Wilson Robinson, for the photographs and family recollections that she has sent across from California in an engaging correspondence. The help of Christine Gladwin, archivist of Sidcot School, was very timely in providing essential information on Janet Robinson. A special word of thanks is due to Barbara Christwitz whose help in locating JWR's relatives in the US was crucial at a particular stage, and the Taliani Group, who guaranteed the quality of the editing. Special thanks are also due to the Fell and Rock Club for permission to use their photographic material, and to their archivist, Iain Whitney, for his help, and to Abraham Photographic for photographs on pages 2, 36, 52, 54 and 59 and to Bob Allen for that on page 20.

Michael Baron, Dennis Hinde, Andrew McClellan, John Stober, Christopher Thomas and Angus Winchester have each made particular contributions, and I should thank also all the people, too numerous to mention, who have given me advice and information in correspondence and conversations. Editorial and technical help have been unstintingly provided by my wife Manon and daughters Nadia and Florence.

Then there are two people, no longer in this world, who I feel have somehow presided over this book. One is Alan Hankinson, whose writings on rock-climbing in the Lake District have achieved the status of an encyclopedia. The other is Edmund Robinson, JWR's brother, who took the trouble in his lifetime to write so much down.

Finally, a word about how the names of places are presented in this book. The names of some fells and locations have changed over time, and it has been decided to use the form that the source used in each case, since this has some historical value. Thus both 'Scafell' and 'Scawfell' appear in the text, and 'Scarth Gap' as well as 'Scarf Gap'. Reference to a current Ordnance Survey map will solve any doubts about today's nomenclature.

CONTENTS

List of illustrations

The building of the Robinson Cairn

Introduction

In the summer of 1881 Walter Parry Haskett-Smith, an undergraduate at Trinity College, Oxford, with already a distinguished record in athletics, visited Wasdale Head in the west of the Lake District, staying in the guest-house of Row Farm. There he divided his time between study for his course in classics and making himself acquainted with the fells. In the following year he returned to Row Farm, this time in the company of a group of friends, and it was on this second visit that he made the remarkable series of climbs that were to establish him as the founder of rock-climbing in the English Lake District. Wasdale Head became at once the hub of the new sport – new in that it engaged the whole body in the conquest of crags that did not necessarily even offer a view from the top. It became as well the centre of a legend, with its mythos of heroes and celebrated achievements.

Amongst those heroes was John Wilson Robinson, the subject of this book. He was not among the visitors to Wasdale Head, his family having lived in the Lake District for centuries. It was, however, in that year of 1882 that he made the acquaintance of Haskett-Smith, and the partnership that formed between them was very much part of the legend of the early years of Lakeland rock-climbing.

The events associated with that emblematic year of 1882, of central importance in the history of sport and of Lakeland society itself, did not arise in a void. The celebration of nature by the Romantic poets, together with the receding of the Scottish threat and improvements in the roads, had led to an incipient tourism even before the coming of the railway to near Windermere in 1847. Moreover, people had in fact been scaling Lakeland crags for a good many years before Haskett-Smith and his companions came to Wasdale Head. The exploits of those earlier climbers had centred on a particular isolated crag, which did not offer itself as a summit for walkers to surmount, but which was peculiarly suited to the new sport. This was Pillar Rock in Ennerdale.

It is in fact unfair that the substantial stream of people who climbed Pillar Rock in the footsteps of the first recorded ascent by the shepherd John Atkinson in 1826 have been thrust into the shadow by the exploits of Haskett-Smith and the Wasdale Head fraternity coming a good deal later. The early Pillarites differed from the Wasdale Head climbers by being drawn for the most part from the Lake District itself and its periphery. One such was George Seatree, from Penrith, who compiled a list of the burgeoning number of ascents of Pillar between 1826 and 1875 – the entire list thus falling before Haskett-Smith's appearance on the scene.

John Wilson Robinson was another of these local figures and a friend of Seatree. Born in 1853 at Whinfell Hall, a yeoman farmstead in the Vale of Lorton, he had tramped the fells from his earliest youth, and had watched the interest in Pillar Rock growing, though it was not until 1882 that he made his own first ascent of it. By then he had already moved from simply walking on the fells to addressing the rock faces and chimneys. He must have followed with interest the developments at Wasdale Head, and it could only have been a matter of time before he made the acquaintance of Haskett-Smith. In addition to his remarkably productive partnership with Haskett-Smith himself, he was to captivate the visitors to Wasdale Head through his skill as a cragsman and his total familiarity with the fells, but perhaps even more by his jovial sociability, his cautious sagacity, and his willingness to devote time and attention to the many younger people who were coming to the rocks to participate in the growing sport.

John Wilson Robinson, or JWR as he will normally be styled in what follows, thus became a key figure in the development of climbing in the English Lake District. On the one hand he benefited from 'being there' at the time when other legendary figures were establishing their climbing credentials as visitors; on the other he had the capacity to make himself one of their number, and one of the most highly regarded of them. When the Fell and Rock Climbing Club was formed in 1906 it was only natural that he should be appointed one of its first Vice-Presidents.

Consequently, in the literature on the heroic period of rock-climbing's formative years, there is an obligatory passage devoted to this dalesman-climber who so fascinated his peers. There has, however, been no attempt yet made to record his life outside the realm of mountaineering. Yet it was this other life that marked him out as different from the visitors, and shaped those aspects of his character that captivated them. It was a life which, had it not been for his climbing record, would no doubt have passed unnoticed by history, yet he was representative of many aspects of the evolution of the Lakes counties in the second half of the nineteenth century. In his lifetime the enclosure of the commons was well advanced, but some of its effects can be illustrated from the structure of Whinfell Hall, his holding . The same is true of the system of customary tenure. He held Whinfell Hall as customary tenant of the lord of the manor of Whinfell, who for much of his life was Baron Leconfield in his castle at Cockermouth. As a yeoman farmer JWR was exposed to the economic difficulties of that class in those years. He was representative also of another social group – the Society of Friends – which has been strong in the Lakes counties since the days of George Fox. Pardshaw, over the fell from Whinfell Hall, where the Robinson family went to Meeting, has played a notable part in the history of the Quakers.

A great deal of Lake District history can therefore be read off from the life and times of John Wilson Robinson, and that is the task addressed in this book. In addition to giving an account of his contribution to rock-climbing it recounts Robinson's personal story. It tells of his Quaker childhood, of his yeoman-farmer family, of the house and farm that comprised Whinfell Hall. It covers also his change in occupation, in his forties, from gentleman farmer to land agent, examining the factors that led to that decision, and its unfortunate sequel.

The book is in two parts. The first – 'The Cragsman' – deals with JWR as a rock-climber. The second part – 'A Dalesman's Life' – situates JWR in the social context of his day. It records also the chain of events that led, by way of some unfortunate financial adventures, to the loss of Whinfell Hall. The first part requires a little explanation. It sets Robinson's exploits on the rocks in the context of the history of climbing in the Lake District in a way that emphasises the social aspects of that history. Readers who are themselves climbers may miss the familiar accounts of how the 'first tigers' (Hankinson's term) conquered crag after crag, climb after climb, over the whole territory of Lakeland. They may wonder why so much attention is being paid to historical matters that seem secondary to the story of climbing. But if these are digressions from the story of climbing itself, they are an integral part of the biography of John Wilson Robinson, and also of the social evolution of the Lake

District of which tourism and mountaineering were so important a part. What is offered here is a study of the life, but also the times, of 'JWR'. There are references in the footnotes to guide readers to the general climbing literature, but the author uses only so much of that literature as illuminates the biographical and historical task.

The question of sources also calls for explanation. The material presented in the first part of the book is drawn largely from the very extensive accounts of the history of climbing. They contain information on JWR both as a cragsman and as a personality. It is important to note, though, that those who have treated him in personal terms have been themselves climbers. The accounts are to that extent partial – not that they have misrepresented him, rather that they have presented the side of his personality that was, as it were, turned to them as climbers.

Unlike the abundance of information on JWR's climbing, that on his life as a yeoman farmer and later land agent is extremely thin. He died childless, his only sister surviving to adulthood also died without offspring, and no personal papers carried by JWR's widow Janet to Shipley after her husband's death are traceable. Such family records as were taken to the United States by his brothers perished in a warehouse fire in Oregon. There are a few short items from his own pen which are to be found in publications of the climbing fraternity. These shed light on his personality, but they say little about the circumstances of his life. The result is that direct sources are almost non-existent. Fortunately, a number of indirect sources have made it possible to write this book.

The first, and most substantial, is a correspondence between JWR's younger brother Edmund in the United States with a certain J.G.Brooker, who was living in Calcutta at the time of the correspondence. Brooker was anxious to know what Edmund could tell him about life around Whinfell in Edmund's youth, and specifically about fellow members of the Society of Friends. From these letters a great deal can be learned about life in the Robinson family at Whinfell Hall in JWR's early years. At the same time, we have the added bonus of information about the Quaker community. This correspondence, bound in two volumes, is held by the Lorton and Derwent Fells Local History Society.

The second source of information is the deeds and papers of Whinfell Hall. These reach back to 1644, and are of inestimable value in illustrating from a particular case the onward march of land enclosure, and the system of customary tenure together with the process of enfranchisement from it. Thirdly, despite the loss of the bulk of the family records taken to the United States, a certain amount survived. It is to JWR's great-grandniece Polly Jones that the author is indebted for the family photographs printed in the book, and also for some letters between JWR and his brothers Edmund and Richard.

Finally, just when it appeared that only vestigial direct information about JWR's wife Janet was ever to be found, the archivist of Sidcot School, where Janet taught before her marriage to JWR, uncovered a series of entries in a collective diary maintained by Janet and a number of her former pupils.

There remain large gaps in our knowledge about the personal life of JWR, and the record has had to be put together as if by stepping-stones, with a degree of inference necessary between the stones. But we know enough to provide a portrait in which the incomplete figure already familiar from the climbing literature can be given a fuller description. It reveals a man in tune with his time in two senses. In his personal life he was a victim of the economic pressures on the Lakeland yeoman farmer, pressures to which he in the end succumbed, to the extent that Whinfell Hall was mortgaged, and could not be redeemed. In his life as a climber he was more fortunate. He was able to take advantage of a new use of his native fells that was developing, to emerge in history as a leading member of the first generation of rock-climbers in the English Lake District. He lost his ancestral home, but he secured for himself a place in the pantheon of climbing legends.

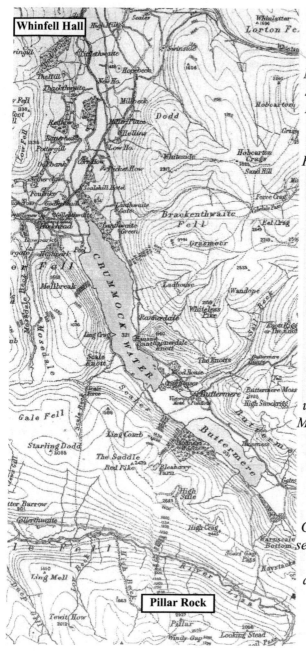

Map from the 1880s showing the Vale of Lorton, Scarth Gap (known then as Scarf Gap) and Pillar Rock. It is not known what route JWR took to reach the Rock, but it is most likely that he went along either the eastern or the western side of Crummock Water, crossing into Ennerdale over Scarth Gap. It is unlikely that he would take the unmarked route up Mosedale if his main aim was to get to Pillar Rock in as short a time as possible. The Nelsons at Gatesgarth used to see of an evening his lantern coming down Scarth Gap.

12

Part One: The Cragsman
Chapter 1: The Creation of a Legend

Whinfell Hall

At four o'clock in the morning - some say even three o'clock - John Wilson Robinson would set off from his farming home at Whinfell Hall near Lorton Bridge in Cumbria and walk the whole length of the Vale of Lorton on foot. Having reached Gatesgarth he would go up and over Scarth Gap into the neighbouring valley of Ennerdale, cross it, and go up the facing fell side until he reached Pillar Rock. There he would spend the main part of the day climbing on that crag with companions who had come up from hostelries at Wasdale Head, before setting off back down the track home to Whinfell Hall. The round trip from Whinfell Hall to the Rock and back was over 20 miles - a good way more when the measurements for ascents are added in. The date was any day in the 15 or so years after 1882.

In that north-western corner of the English Lake District the river Cocker flows from Crummock Water down the Vale of Lorton to join the river Derwent at Cockermouth, a distance of six miles as the crow flies, though somewhat more as the water flows. The river is bridged shortly after it leaves the lake, and again at rather less than half its length in the village of Lorton, by which point the valley has broadened out to over a mile wide. The fells around Lorton, with one exception, are of modest height and are not part of the igneous dome of the central Lake District. The exception is Hopegill Head and the horseshoe around it, which give an intimation of what lies higher up the valley, for around Crummock Water, and increasingly around Buttermere, which is separated from Crummock by a short stretch of ground, the valley necks sharply in and the surrounding fells – Red Pike, High Stile, Fleetwith Pike, Dale Head and Robinson - rise to heights of over 2000 feet, and 2790 for the massive Grassmoor. If crags can be said to beetle, those around Buttermere certainly do.

Over against Hopegill Head in the gentler part of the lower valley, and across the Cocker, lies a long low fell, more than a hill but much less than a mountain, forming the opposing flank of the Vale of Lorton. This, historically, was Whin Fell, though today it is known by a variety of names, some attaching to the whole low range – Low Fell, Mosser Fell – others to its various high points. According to local tradition the fell got its name of Whinfell from the whins, or gorse, which grew in abundance on it. Nestling at its foot, hard by the bridge, lies a small hamlet, today comprising four dwellings and a substantial barn, together with a campsite and its associated facilities. The name 'Whinfell Hall' now attaches to only one of the houses, but this book concerns a time when the entire collection of buildings together with a considerable surrounding acreage was an integrated homestead. It was here that John Wilson Robinson was born on 5 August 1853, the eldest son of the yeoman farmer who ran Whinfell Hall. He was to run it himself for most of his adult life, whilst making time to play a prominent role in the development of rock-climbing in the English Lake District.

It is a feature of the Lake District that the term 'hall' has been used historically in this way. The simplicity of many of Lakeland's 'halls' seems to conflict with understandings in other parts of the country, where a hall is expected to display a certain grandeur. There is, in fact, less of a conflict than might at first appear. Grandeur is a relative concept. There were gentry in the valley, in the sense of individual well-off people in substantial houses who lived elegantly – more elegantly than the yeoman Robinsons, who lived more simply than the gentry because of their Quaker convictions, yet who were given the title of 'gentleman' on many a deed or other legal document. But there was no land-owning squirearchy of the kind to be found further south and which provided the model for the novels of Sterne, Fielding or Dickens, with the livings of clergymen and the ownership of whole villages vested in the squire. In these Lakeland circumstances the term 'hall' was used to connote any large farmstead with its outbuildings and dependencies.

In medieval times Whinfell Hall was included in the 'township' of Whinfell. This grouped a string of homesteads which lay in a crescent round the foot of the low fell from which the township took its name, starting a mile up the valley from Whinfell Hall, running along it northwards and curving right round through Rogerscale and Toddell to end at Aikbank Mill, by which point the Vale of Lorton has been left behind and the view is westward towards the coastal plain.

The township of Whinfell thus lay over the river from the village of Lorton, which was itself a distinct township. Further, in John Wilson Robinson's time, Whinfell lay within the parish of Brigham, which was likewise separated from the parish of Lorton by the river Cocker. It was not, in any case, to Brigham church, let alone to St Cuthbert's, the parish church in Lorton, that the Robinson family went to practice their religious observance, but to the Quaker Meeting House at Pardshaw, which lay over the fell behind the homestead. This is matter for a later chapter, but it is worth noting here that Pardshaw has played an important part in the history of the Society of Friends and that the Friends were strongly implanted in the Lakes counties in general.

Finally, Whinfell was separated from Lorton by another legacy of medieval times, the manor. Whinfell Hall lay, appropriately enough, in the manor of Whinfell, which in medieval times was a 'parcel' of the 'honour' of Cockermouth. We shall see that it was to Lord Leconfield in his castle in Cockermouth that JWR paid rent as 'customary tenant' of Whinfell Hall in the manor of Whinfell.

As late as 1868, when JWR was 13 years old, the *National Gazetteer* listed Whinfell as a township within the parish of Brigham, which in turn was within the honour of Cockermouth. By then, however, these features of earlier times had considerably evolved and were to continue to evolve during JWR's lifetime. Customary tenure of land had become virtual freehold, while the medieval townships went with the major reform of local government that culminated in the County Councils Act of 1888. Parish boundaries continued to set Whinfell apart from Lorton, but the separation was vestigial, and Lorton was the community within which JWR's life was lived – with the noted exception of religious observance.

Wasdale Head

One of the companions with whom JWR climbed on Pillar Rock at the end of his long walk to the spot was Walter Parry Haskett-Smith who, at the time when he met JWR, was an undergraduate at Trinity College, Oxford. Haskett-Smith is conventionally regarded as the founder of rock-

The Wastwater Hotel in 1889

climbing in England, but it is the joint contribution of the dalesman and the undergraduate, and the social contrast between them, that has provided the stuff of the legend that unites them in the history of climbing in the Lake District.

In 1880 Haskett-Smith had gone with a group of fellow undergraduates to Snowdonia, combining reading with walking. It was in the next summer, of 1881, that he made his acquaintance with the Lake District, staying for four weeks at Wasdale Head in rooms at Row Farm guesthouse. By that date Row Farm was one of two hostelries at Wasdale Head catering for the increasing number of visitors to the Lake District – or rather to a particular group of them, those for whom the central fells held a particular attraction, with a strong representation of people on vacation from the universities. Lower down the valley from Row Farm

Will Ritson and his wife Dinah had in 1856 acquired a licence to dispense alcoholic beverages in their farmhouse and opened part of it to visitors under the name of the Huntsman's Inn, later to be renamed the Wastwater Hotel.

The record abounds with graphic stories about Will Ritson. He was, after all, in constant contact with his guests, who were not slow to pick up, store and relate folkloric tales about their Cumbrian host. Alan Hankinson tells of his boast that Wasdale had the 'highest mountain in England, the deepest lake, the smallest church, and the biggest liar'. In this humble listing, Ritson claimed the slot of biggest liar, but 'the lees Aa tell isn't malicious; they're nobbut gert big exaggerations'.[1] It was, however, a fellow Cumbrian who told how, when asked why he settled in Wasdale Head, Ritson had said that when he first came into the valley he saw an old man crying, and asked for the reason. The old man replied that his father had just whipped him. And the reason for that? For throwing stones at his grandfather. Ritson concluded that there was something to be said for living in a place where people maintained their vigour to such a great age.[2]

Row Farm offered a rather different atmosphere from the Huntsman's Inn/Wastwater Hotel. It was smaller, teetotal, and was run by Tom and Annie Tyson (no relation of Dan Tyson who succeeded Will Ritson as landlord of the Huntsman's Inn). If the chief attraction at the Huntsman's was the boisterous Will Ritson, Row Farm was best prized for Annie Tyson's cooking. It was the Wastwater Hotel that was to become the main base of the rock-climbing fraternity after Haskett-Smith's second visit to Wasdale Head in 1882.

Whatever their relative merits in terms of accommodation, these two hostelries can claim the historical honour of having catered for a clientele that was changing the face of English sport, and with that the social character of the Lake District. In terms of social history, hostelries are like buses or hermit crabs. They are a shell with a constantly shifting content. Haskett-Smith and his like were but the latest in a changing clientele of visitors, from those who had come to indulge a fascination with nature bred of the Romantic movement, to a brief generation of Alpine mountaineers who came to the Lake District in winter to practice techniques of climbing on ice that could be applied on the larger summits of ranges abroad. By the 1880s, however, most of the Alpine peaks had been conquered; there was room for diversity in the goals of those with a taste for confronting rocky challenges.

Much of this evolving clientele shared a common feature, in being drawn from the universities, which in that day still meant Oxford or Cambridge. True, the establishment of University College London in 1826 had been followed in the second half of the century by the creation of the major civic universities. But this expansion of the student body had not yet seriously modified the prevailing patterns of social behaviour, nor had it put sufficient money into pockets to pay for extended holiday accommodation, and the day of mass camping was yet to dawn. It is not incidental that the classical 'Greats' degree that Haskett-Smith took at Oxford was the favoured background for a career in the Indian civil service in those colonial days.

It was through the medium of such visitors, particularly numerous at Wasdale Head, that simply walking on the hills, already a favourite vacation pastime of a previous generation of Varsity folk, grew into the sport of rock-climbing. That in turn followed its own development, its adepts first conquering crags unattached to one another by whatever route offered itself, then took more structured form with a study of routes and with the adoption of the climbing rope to give security – a theme to which we return below.

JWR made Haskett-Smith's acquaintance in 1884, and a partnership soon developed between them. It formed to a great extent around their activities on a particular crag, designed as if by nature to offer a terrain for the new sport of climbing on rocks. It was already a legend in itself as a result of the competition to climb it that had grown up after the first recorded ascent in 1826. That crag was Pillar Rock.

Pillar Rock

Pillar Rock, or Pillar Stone as it was called when our chronicle begins, lies on the flank of the mountain Pillar at the head of Ennerdale in the north-western segment of the Lake District. It is detached from the mountain and rises to a height of some 500 feet from its base on Pillar's northern side, a chaotic area of scree, crags and fallen boulders. It is claimed to be the highest more or less vertical crag in England, yet at the same time it is one of the least visited by the general run of visitors to the Lake District, being probably unknown to the majority of them.

There are a number of reasons for this paradox, as A.H.Griffin points out in his *Inside the Real Lake District*. First, Ennerdale itself is one of the least attractive valleys of the Lake District. There is access by road only to the foot of the valley and the long path onward is fairly dreary. Second, if you approach Ennerdale over Scarth Gap, which is the pass giving a frontal view of Pillar Mountain, Pillar Rock can only with difficulty be picked out by the eye from the mountain's side, nor does it reveal itself to a walker continuing on across the head of the valley to the Black Sail Pass on the other side, since from there the Rock is a good way off to the right. Third, although the Rock itself is high as a single crag it is not high enough to be part of the panorama of peaks visible from the major summits. Finally, from the top of Pillar Mountain itself the Rock appears quite insignificant

However, for those who persevere and arrive at the Rock its majesty is breath-taking. George Abraham, saluting its verticality and the deep fissures that are one of its most striking features, marvelled at its 'organ-pipe cliffs'. For George Seatree it was '...more like some vast cathedral pile than a "pillar stone"'; for E Lynn Linton it was 'a great grey striated column which fires all one's ambition to surmount [it]'.[3] In perhaps the most graphic image of all, a writer to the *West Cumberland News* in November 1884 wrote:

> The spell which this rock throws over the minds of those who have visited it is enthralling. It is of the nature of a psychological mystery not to be accounted for on ordinary grounds. It is strange. The Pillar Rock is merely a mass of crags with no inherent difference from other masses save that it juts up boldly ... from the precipitous breast of Pillar Mountain. Yet, once seen, it is the lodestone to the pieces of iron in the story of the Third Royal Calender.[4]

A.H.Griffin's description is as follows:

> It rises straight ahead (from the High-Level Route which skirts Pillar Mountain), a great cathedral-like structure, but bigger than any cathedral in the world. A green ledge runs along its foot and above it the great walls rise almost vertically for about five hundred feet to Low Man, above which there is an upper section a few hundred feet in height leading to High Man, the small summit. The crag is

The west face of Pillar Rock

flanked by other crags, with scree slopes in between, and there are only a few places in Britain – all of them in Scotland – where you can see more rock in one glance.

Viewed from this point, it is easy to understand why the Rock has always been an object of awe to the surrounding dales-folk. An elderly dalesman recorded by H.M.Kelly and W.Peascod put the matter in briefer but no less effective form. Standing gazing up, with his wife, at the great sweep of cliff before them he said simply, 'Aye, it's a grand stone'.

Pillar Rock has exercised a fascination on rock-climbers since the birth of the sport, offering them a terrain that they know is effectively theirs alone. Wainwright's *Pictorial Guide to the Lakeland Fells* offers a stern warning to others:

> To walkers whose experience is limited to easy scrambling on rough ground, Pillar Rock is positively out of bounds. Don't even try to get a foothold on it. The climbing guides mention easy routes ... but these are NOT easy for a walker who is not a climber, and lead into dangerous situations.

He adds: 'Remember the stretcher-box'. An anonymous 'member of the Alpine Club' put the same sentiment in other terms in a letter to the editor of the *Visitor and Guardian* on the difficulties of climbing on Pillar Rock: 'You can always make a fool of yourself when life has lost all charms for you; why be in a hurry to do so now?'

* * *

So it was that John Wilson Robinson, Walter Haskett-Smith and Pillar Rock came to be linked together as symbols of one particular aspect of social change at one particular time in one particular part of the north of England, and it was around Whinfell Hall, Wasdale Head and Pillar Rock that a legend came to be formed. Within that legend JWR stands out as a local dalesman, in a sport that was being created to a great extent by visitors to the Lake District. In the record JWR is therefore seen from outside, by others, who were impressed, fascinated but bemused by the dalesman. To explore the legend, and to discover the full contours of the life of a man at its heart three avenues are worth opening up. The first is the way in which rock-climbing was born in the England of JWR's day. The second is the story of Pillar Rock and JWR's special relationship with it. The third is the life story of JWR himself on his farm, and later as a land agent.

In the next chapter the first of these avenues will be followed.

1 Hankinson, Alan, *A Century on the Crags: The Story of Rock-Climbing in the English Lake District*, Striding Edge, 1997, p. 25

2 *Extracts from Letters Written by Edmund Robinson late of Whinfell Hall to J.G. Brooker 1931-1943*, typescript, Lorton and Derwent Fells Local History Society archive, p.78.

3 Seatree, George, 'Reminiscences of early Lakeland mountaineering', *Fell and Rock Climbing Club Journal*, 2:1, 1910, p.10; Linton, E Lynn, *The Lake Country*, cited in Nicholson, N. *The Lake District: An Anthology*, p.64.

4 The reference is to the story in the Arabian Nights of the third calender (or kalandar) with his description of a mountain, whose magnetic force was so great that the iron and nails were drawn out of passing ships and stuck to the mountain.

Chapter 2:
The Birth of Climbing in the Lake District

A good time before the visits of Haskett-Smith and his companions to Wasdale Head at the beginning of the 1880s the paths had become established that took walkers to the summits of the fells, and by then, too, there were many who had taken to scaling crags simply for the sport of it, thus sowing the seeds for what was to come later. But it was not until the 1880s that those seeds matured.

John Wilson Robinson was one of the most intriguing of the legendary figures of the creative period that ensued. He is not accorded a great deal of space in the written accounts of the early years, yet he is treated with a very special respect. This derives from two sources. First, he fell ill and died in 1907 aged only 54 at the very moment when the Fell and Rock Climbing Club was being formed, and he had just been designated a joint Vice-President of it. JWR's sudden disappearance at that point, and the closing of the book on the life of one of climbing's early heroes, invested the memory of JWR with something akin to a martyr's mantle. But the respect with which JWR has been treated has a more substantial cause. He knew the Lakeland fells intimately. Tramping them was already his life before scaling rocks became part of it. In this he was different from the band of visitors who made Wasdale Head their base for one or two months in the year.

To understand what it means to call those years legendary, and what marks them out as a period of historical importance, some of the social background to them must be filled in. The narrative then returns, with an introduction to three people, companions of JWR on the rocks, who illustrate the circumstances in which the sport of climbing came to the Lake District, drawing in the yeoman farmer who is the chief focus of this book.

As the Industrial Revolution got under way a number of factors impeded the general economic progress of Cumberland in relation to other parts of the country. It was relatively remote from markets of any size and from the areas of greatest social change at a time when England was experiencing both the benefits and the costs of industrial development and colonialism. Second, although the formal union of Scotland and England had been achieved with the Act of 1707, the memory of border raids and overall insecurity remained in people's minds long thereafter. There was also the fact that the region's mountainous nature and bad roads made access to it and travel within it difficult until well into the nineteenth century. There were periods of relative prosperity in differing parts of the region (the tonnage of shipping outward from Whitehaven for a time in the eighteenth century surpassed that from Liverpool, Bristol or Newcastle, for example), but the centre of gravity in the overall industrial map of England was to be established to the south. The basis of an earlier industrial strength – the mining of the Elizabethan Company of the Mines Royal, the woollen industry of Kendal, the iron-smelting bloomeries of Furness, and the fulling mills — disappeared into history.

Lakeland's future, and particularly that of the fells and valleys of its heartland, was to be guaranteed by a new economic activity – tourism. This developed in two distinct periods, with the coming of the railway as a clear turning point.

In the first period incipient tourism merged with a rising appreciation of the Lakeland landscape by people already living there. The eighteenth century had seen important advances in road-building which, taken together with the receding of the Scottish problem, opened up the Lakes counties to travellers. This had obvious economic benefits, but by one of the coincidences of history this improved accessibility came at a time when the Romantic movement in English art and literature was in gestation. It was the pre-Romantic Thomas Gray whose *Journal in the Lakes* of 1775 is usually taken to have struck the first note in this appreciation of the Lakeland landscape and way of life, his detailed observation of nature accompanied by a quaintly idealistic approval of the 'peace, rusticity and happy poverty' that he encountered. Only a few years later the first guide-book for visitors was published, though it took some time for the existing association of the Lake District with gloomy forbidding valleys and frightening crags best avoided by travellers to dissipate. A taste for mountain scenery developed, congenial to the spirit of romanticism, and the way lay open to the emergence of the Lake District as a prime destination for those with the time and the money to enjoy its peace and its natural beauty.

It was concern for its natural beauty that led William Wordsworth to be outspoken in his distress at the development of tourism in the Lake District, even before the coming of the railway. That important turning-point was reached in 1847, when a branch was opened westwards from the main Lancaster to Carlisle line, terminating (it was thought provisionally at the time) at what is now Windermere, but was then the hamlet of Birthwaite, a little over a mile above Bowness and the lake. Eighteen years later the line through Keswick to Cockermouth was completed.

Interestingly, Wordsworth chooses Pillar Rock as the setting of his poem *The Brothers,* written in 1800, which illustrates well the contempt that the poet felt for the visitors who were appearing even at that early date. In the poem, a Lakeland 'Priest' addresses his wife who, with her husband, was 'engaged in winter's work' - she teasing matted wool, he feeding it to the spindle of his youngest child, and Wordsworth sets these wholesome activities against the predilections of the visitor

> ... who needs must leave the path
> Of the world's business to go wild alone:
> His arms have a perpetual holiday;
> The happy man will creep about the fields,
> Following his fancies by the hour, to bring
> Tears down his cheek, or solitary smiles
> Into his face, until the setting sun
> Write Fool upon his forehead.

One man's fancies are another man's poetry, but in any case Wordsworth and those who thought like him were overtaken by history. People were coming to the Lake District in increasing numbers, and the laying of sleepers and rails was only one factor promoting social change. The railway would not have been built had there not been an increase in the time people had to ride on it, or in the money they had to buy a ticket.

This massive leap in its accessibility to wider sections of the population transformed the economic fortunes of the Lake District, turning its resident population into a minority in relation to the great numbers of passing visitors, as well as radically changing the make-up of the resident population itself. The change was particularly felt in the major resort towns of Windermere (with Bowness), Ambleside and Keswick. In the central fells, change came more slowly. The railheads and metalled roads that brought visitors in great numbers to the major holiday destinations cannot have very much facilitated the journey of the likes of Haskett-Smith, who still had to cover a good part of their trek to Wasdale Head by horse-drawn transport.

To situate the development of rock-climbing within the overall evolution of tourism in the Lake District in the later part of the nineteenth century is not a simple matter. For example, in their study of the Lakes counties of the time, Marshall and Walton point out that Wasdale and Ennerdale were particularly sluggish in their provision of accommodation, while specifically mentioning Ritson and the Huntsman's Inn – 'These western lakes were unique in their continuing isolation from the main tourist centres'.[1] In fact, given the difficulty of getting to the central fells, the history of rock climbing benefited only tangentially from the coming of mass tourism in more accessible areas. In the 1880s it had no mass character and depended not so much on the railways as on the geography of a particular part of the Lake District. Nevertheless, the factors that were generating mass tourism were certainly playing a part in introducing to the Lake District the visitors of the 1880s, who were to give a new impetus to the earliest shoots of Lakeland rock-climbing (we encounter these in the next chapter).

Rock-climbing, in any case, benefited greatly from other social developments of the time. The England of Victoria was not only generating the material factors that opened the Lake District to visitors. It also produced a set of values and patterns of behaviour characteristic of that period which strongly influenced the development of sport. A new vision of sporting activity required that the barbarity and dishonest manipulation of the past be set aside and moral qualities encouraged. A shift consequently took place from spectator sports – pugilistics, bear-baiting and cock-fighting, where the barbarity lay – to competition. 'A zest for annihilation gave way to a taste for contention and emulation, as the Victorians discovered that sport could be equated with virtue'.[2] The ethic that emerged has been known to some historians as 'muscular Christianity'.

Growing notions of self-improvement meant that competition could be viewed as the testing of the self both against others and against what one had achieved up to that point. This was the period when, in 1859, Samuel Smiles published his influential book *Self-help*. The changing values were strongly marked by distinctions of class and, given the circumstances, it was in the expansion of the urban middle class that they were chiefly reflected. Lowerson has pointed out that when these new groups 'rather belatedly' turned to sport it was to those sports that allowed ethical purity to be displayed and the inner self tested.[3] The role of the public schools, which in turn fed the Universities, Oxford and Cambridge in particular, in the inculcation of the new values, has frequently been recorded. It was bolstered by the more material consideration that the risk of infections spreading in the dense living conditions of a boarding school could be diminished by a diet of health-promoting sport.

In this context newer forms of sport took on a middle-class character. This was not, of course, to last in the case of rock-climbing. As it developed on the Cumbrian fells after JWR's generation, and as the increase in leisure time and ease of travel continued to expand, rock-climbing came to be marked precisely by its lack of class, and gender, distinctions. The rocks are great levelers, and the camaraderie of a mountain hut, youth hostel, or pub outweighs social differences. Also, the fact that climbers were exercising their skills away from their home environment meant that they were free from the social hang-ups that English society has been prone to. Even in JWR's time climbing differed from the more general development of sport in Victorian England in being free of the clash between the professional and the amateur, as witnessed in an extreme case by the way in which rowing became cocooned by class, with competitions among professional boatmen being severely segregated from the amateur races of middle- or upper-class 'oarsmen'.

In the circumstances of the time it was a natural development that reading parties from the universities should travel during the vacation to the mountains of the Lake District and divide the time they spent there between developing the mind and the body in surroundings whose wholesomeness had been sung by the Romantic poets. Equally understandable was the spirit of competition – against self, against others and against the rocks - that was to develop as the bodily side of that equation began to map out a sporting terrain for rivalry within a group of like-minded spirits.

At the same time, it must be realised that, as so often in European affairs, the various countries of the continent were showing broadly similar patterns of social change. Whilst there is something irreducibly English about 'Victorian values', they cannot in themselves alone be held to have provided the spur for the development of rock-climbing. In his book *Big Wall Climbing,* Doug Scott points out that in Germany and Austria, no less than in England, young people were taking to scaling rocks in much the same way, for much the same reasons, and at exactly the same time as Haskett-Smith and his fellow visitors to Wasdale Head.

These developments can be illustrated through three of JWR's closest companions on the rocks, each of them revealing a particular aspect of the history of rock-climbing in the Lakes. Frederick Bowring, a Cambridge law don, can be held up as an example of continuity with the Romantic period and with the people who from the start of the nineteenth century had come to the Lakes to enjoy the natural features of that environment. Walter Haskett-Smith stands as the most prominent case of the younger generation of Victorians whose visits to the Lakes on vacation spearheaded the development of rock-climbing in Lakeland (picking up Bowring in the process). George Seatree was a Cumbrian who, like JWR, represented a local interest in rock-climbing which had taken Pillar Rock for its focus of activity even before the landmark date of Haskett-Smith's second visit to Wasdale Head in 1882. These three figures have not been selected here as the leading 'tigers' of the early years, though of course Haskett-Smith certainly was one of them. The aim is rather to illustrate the context in which rock climbing developed, and to situate JWR among its early exponents.

Frederick Hermann Bowring was already 30 years old when JWR was born, and was in his fifties by the time they met. He was the son of Sir John Bowring, who was active in the Anti-Corn Law League and served as MP for Bolton before being appointed Plenipotentiary to China and then Governor of Hong Kong. Frederick studied at Trinity College, Cambridge, with his father's prudential blessing: 'You will therefore go to Cambridge in a thoughtful studious way…to distinguish yourself by application of intelligence and to lay the foundations for honourable recompense in after life'. The family home was near Exeter, and Frederick

F. H. Bowring

made frequent visits to Dartmoor when he was on vacation, and later too when he had secured a fellowship in law at Trinity College at the ripe old age of 26. He had visited North Wales in 1849, but not even on Snowdon had he felt 'anything so fresh, so bracing without being cold, in a word so health-bringing as the September air on these Dartmoor wastes'. He lived in Lincoln's Inn in London in this early period of his life, which his visiting fellowship in Cambridge allowed, but even in London (which he called 'the boiling, raging central pulse of the world') he walked for at least an hour each day, weather permitting, usually around St. James's Park.

His diaries reveal him as a solitary, scholarly lawyer. Readings in the bible ('in German, Spanish, Italian, Serbian' he noted in his diary for 30 January 1853) were a daily routine, taking from one to one-and-a-half hours of his mornings. Visits were from relatives and professional colleagues, often involving a game of chess, each gambit played being carefully recorded. Feminine company gets scant mention. 'Dinner from six to ten. A Miss Farmer there, petite but very pretty – manners not good perhaps but apparently a nice girl. Did not speak to her however', he records on one occasion. Each daily entry begins with a detailed statement about the weather, including the direction of the wind. He fumes when the rain prevents him from his long walks in the park.

From early times his readings point him in the direction of the Lake District. Significantly, he discusses Wordsworth in his correspondence with his father. He reads Coleridge, and de Quincey. The date of Bowring's first visit to the Lakes is not recorded, but we know from JWR's *Diary* that he made his hundredth ascent of Gable on 15 June 1885. Clearly his familiarity with the Lakes must have been of long standing.

It was when he was ensconced in Row Farm in Wasdale Head in the summer of 1881 that he made the acquaintance of the young Walter Haskett-Smith, who was on his first visit to the Lakes. The two formed an immediate friendship. The next year saw them both at Wasdale Head again, climbing together on Pillar Rock and Scafell. Bowring's encounter with this member of the new generation that was to launch the sport of rock-climbing in the Lake District must have had an immensely reinvigorating effect on him, giving this walker of the Romantic period a second life as a rock-climber.

Walter Parry Haskett-Smith

George Seatree

Haskett-Smith himself was born to a land-owning family in Kent. He spent his school years at Eton before going up to Trinity College in Oxford. When he met Bowring during his 1881 visit to Row Farm he was in the third year of a four-year course. Coming to Wasdale Head again in the following year with three Oxford friends and his younger brother, he began to open up the climbing routes that would establish him as the father of rock-climbing in the English Lake District. A list of first ascents compiled by H.M.Kelly and J.H.Doughty in the mid-1930s shows that of the 20 made in the decade from the beginning of 1882 to the end of 1892, he was responsible for all but five. Apart from his individual climbing record, he is representative of the association that was to form between Wasdale Head and the series of visitors with academic or professional backgrounds who were so influential in the history of climbing in the Lakes in its early years. These few words will serve as an introduction to a figure who will feature in many places in this biography as it proceeds.

JWR first met Walter Haskett-Smith and Frederick Bowring, together, in 1884 in unusual circumstances. An accident had taken place on the ground between Mickledore and Broad Stand on Scafell, when a young medical student from Edinburgh named Petty fell 100 feet onto the scree below Mickledore and was very badly injured. JWR, who was nearby at the time, helped get Petty to Burnthwaite at the head of Wasdale where a surgeon who happened to be staying there was able to patch him up. When after two weeks the injured climber was fit to go home, JWR came over from Whinfell Hall to help move him and was met on Sty Head by Bowring and Haskett-Smith. The recuperating climber was picked up and transported by wheelbarrow to the road, where he could be put into a carriage.

It was in this way that the celebrated partnership between JWR and Haskett-Smith was born, with Bowring present at the birth. Contact once made on this occasion in 1884, the partnership was cemented in the days that followed, and was to deepen over the following two decades. Such social differences as there were between them counted for nothing on the rocks. The partnership, however, was a broader affair than scaling particular rocks. It was expressed just as much in their simply going about together over the fells and sizing up possible climbs.

A notable case was their exploration of the Wasdale face of Great

Gable in 1884, which was to lead to the first ascent of Napes Needle. Two years earlier Haskett-Smith had chanced to notice from afar 'a slender pinnacle of rock' rising solitary from that flank of Gable. The pinnacle was no stranger to JWR. His father had come across it many years earlier and had made a sketch of it. JWR therefore had an idea of what to look for as he and Haskett-Smith passed over the screes. He was none the less delighted when they came upon the Needle and, according to his companion, 'inquired whether any Swiss guide would be ready to tackle such a thing'. They themselves passed it by on this occasion, and it was not until two years later that Haskett-Smith made his celebrated ascent of the Needle, alone, having thrown some stones up to determine whether its top was flat or rounded – and having left his handkerchief fluttering on the summit as a marker of his feat. JWR himself was to be the fourth cragsman to climb Napes Needle, on 12 August 1889, taking W.A.Wilson with him.

George Seatree wrote of the partnership between Haskett-Smith and JWR: 'It was good for Lake District climbing that these two ardent pioneers should have met so early and become fast friends and colleagues. They were essential to each other. The local knowledge and keenness of the one, with the dash and skill of the other, and the enthusiasm and safeness of both, formed them into a powerful combination for conquest'.[4]

George Seatree's own particular role in the early history of rock-climbing in the Lake District was that of chronicler of the events of the formative period. He was close to JWR, and without his writing about the relationship this book could hardly have been written. But his pen served a wider purpose, and a good deal of the contemporary record of climbing in the Lake District was his work. When the Fell and Rock Climbing Club was formed in 1907 he was appointed, with JWR, a joint Vice-President, and the pages of the early issues of its journal carry frequent articles written by him, some under his name, others anonymous.

Despite the historical resonance of the later partnership with Haskett-Smith, it was with Seatree that JWR first made his acquaintance of the rocks. Seatree was born in Penrith in 1851, the youngest of a large family. His father had worked as a lead miner at Alston Moor, but launched out on his own with a haulage business before opening a flour mill. The young

Napes Needle.
When JWR and Haskett-Smith first looked at the Needle as a climbing
challenge in 1884, JWR was already familiar with it from a sketch his
father had drawn. It was two years later that Haskett-Smith made the
celebrated first ascent of the Needle, on his own. The female figure on
the summit is believed to be George Seatree's daughter Evelyn.

JWR and George Seatree on their camping trip.

George helped in the mill, but his heart was in politics, supporting the reform movement of those vibrant years. We find him pelting opposition speakers with dolly-blue bags in the 1868 elections in East Cumberland, and spending a martyr's hour or two in the cells. Aged 22, he emigrated to Canada, opening a store there, but returned after two years, to become active again in Liberal associations in Penrith and at county level. On his father's death in 1886 he moved to Liverpool, then to Bootle, remaining very active in politics in support of Gladstone's Home Rule Bill.

History will know him better, however, as a pioneer of rock-climbing in the Lake District. Although Pillar Rock came to be associated particularly with JWR in the annals of the sport, Seatree had already climbed the rock before he met JWR, and he went on to chronicle the early ascents made before and after that date. His devotion to Pillar was whole-hearted. He treated it as a sort of shrine, and indeed the greater part of our knowledge of the early history of his beloved crag is due to the care and foresight with which he collected every scrap of information relating to it. We return to this theme in the next chapter.

He had first reconnoitred the Rock (at the time known as the 'Pillar Stone') with a Penrith friend on Good Friday 1874 'to find out for ourselves all we could of...the whereabouts and character of the Ennerdale Pillar Stone'. It was very shortly after this that he met JWR while in Cockermouth on a business visit. Both being 'natives' ('la'al paddock' –little frog – was Seatree's nickname among his climbing friends) they had much in common apart from their genuine love for the fells, and a close association very soon grew up between them. By that time Seatree had embraced rock-climbing as a sport. JWR had not, his remarkable familiarity with the fells deriving simply from tramping them from an early age. To that extent it was Seatree who introduced JWR to rock-climbing as such, though there is every reason to expect JWR to have been aware, through press reports and conversations, of the new activities that were developing around him.

In 1885, eleven years after their landmark first meeting, Seatree and JWR made a camping trip together. An account of the trip left by Robinson himself in a series of letters to Fred W. Jackson, published some time after JWR's death in the *Journal* of the Fell and Rock Climbing Club, has become a celebrated document in the annals of climbing. It illustrates well JWR's style as a *raconteur,* the sense of drama that went with it, and also the awe and respect that he felt towards accidents on the rocks. For these reasons it is worth giving some details of it.

The trip lasted a week, from a Tuesday in June to the following Monday. The first day was spent on Pillar Rock, trying various routes. 'Then to camp and made the porridge', wrote JWR,

We were ready for it, but oh Seatree you have forgotten the salt, surely we have earned it. However, we stirred some in and made a hearty meal. All campers say you don't sleep the first night and so we found it – it was never dark, we told stories and at 12 o'clock turned out to see the grand old crags, the wind moaned among the Pillar Gullies and slight rain showers began to fall. We lit our candle and read a leader in the Standard … Oh, how uneven this ground is, we will have a better place next night, and do you know this will be a watercourse if it comes a thunderstorm.

The next night's 'better place' was Wasdale Head, which remained their base. On the Saturday, they received a visit from the farmer who was impressed to find our pair writing letters: 'Well I nivver seed letters written i' this field a'foor. What he's just writtin them off and chucking them ower his shoulder in'ter dyke back, if you go on a larl bit langer dyke back will be full'. Returning the next day he remarked: 'Well, you hevn't started writin letters yet. You mun hev a rest as its Sunday'.

It is of some historical interest, from the point of view of climbing equipment, that both JWR and Seatree followed a declining convention by walking with fell-poles (see page X). Also of interest, in relation to today's transport system, is that when the pair departed from Wasdale Head, they left their equipment to be sent back - by rail!

Of the three climbing companions of JWR presented here on account of their historical role in the birth of rock-climbing in the Lakes, it was probably with Seatree that JWR had the closest personal friendship. After JWR's untimely death in 1907, it was Seatree who contributed the main written tributes to the deceased cragsman, and took the lead in having a memorial plaque to him placed near Pillar Rock. It is hard to judge to what extent sentiment counted in the formidable climbing partnership with Haskett-Smith, though it cannot have been small. JWR's relationship with Bowring was one simply of companionship on the rocks.

It was only to be expected that the burgeoning activity around Wasdale Head in the last two decades of the nineteenth century would have engendered calls for the creation of an organisation of Lakeland climbers, a ring to bind them all. It was not until 1906, however, that the idea of forming an association took practical shape.

The story of the Club's founding is told by an anonymous chronicler in the first number of the *Journal* that the Club published in 1907. The role of prime movers is attributed to E.H.P Scantlebury and Alan Craig, and the key moment was an informal meeting held in the Smoke Room of the Sun Hotel in Coniston on 11 November 1906.

A steering-committee was appointed and given the task of drawing up a circular letter in the form of a prospectus to be sent to known mountaineers and others sympathetic to the aims of the proposed association as stated in the circular. Having elicited an encouraging response, the committee addressed the business of endowing the association with an organisational framework. In anticipation of a first general meeting to give the measures effect, it was proposed that the name 'Fell and Rock Club of the English Lake District' be adopted, that officers be appointed and a set of rules drawn up. The prospectus emphasised the 'desirability of, and the advantages accruing from a purely local Club, organised, officered, and managed mainly by men residing within its own borders', and it was in keeping with this preference that Ashley Abraham of Keswick was appointed President, with JWR and George Seatree as joint Vice-Presidents. Ashley Abraham was one of two photographer brothers, either of whom could have served as well as Seatree as representatives of the local climbing fraternity. Suitable patronage for the new venture was assured by inviting to serve as Honorary Members eleven further figures known for their distinguished climbing record or notable services to mountaineering: Cecil Slingsby, Walter Haskett-Smith, Norman Collie, Charles Pilkington, Geoffrey Hastings, L.R.Wilberforce, George Abraham (Ashley's brother), H.D.Rawnsley, C.A.O.Baumgartner, George Bryant and J.Nelson Burrows.

The first General Meeting of the Club was convened for Easter Saturday, 30 March 1907, when its first officially arranged outing was due to take place. It was attended by thirteen out of the membership of 120 that the Club had reached by that time. A revised prospectus spelled out the reasons for the Club's formation. While it spoke of the 'real need' for creating an association, it did not give the Club the practical mission of representing a mountaineering interest in the public arena, but dwelt rather on mutual support and togetherness:

> It has been felt that pedestrians, mountaineers, and rock climbers, living either within the borders of the district or beyond, would be all the better for coming together and for the possession of greater facilities for cultivating each other's friendship, also for opportunities to render mutual assistance in the enjoyable exercise of their sport over our delightful Northern 'playground'.

On one point, however, it was very practical. The first of its stated objects was 'to encourage and foster under the safest and most helpful conditions the exhilarating exercise and sport of fell rambling and rock-climbing in the Lake District'. This was in fact the moment that was bound to arise when the risks that naturally attended the new-born sport of rock-climbing began to take their toll. It must be remembered that in those early days the risks were increased by the burden of loose rock and untested surfaces that the crags carried. Accidents accumulated fairly soon to a critical mass. A number of the early examples were particularly dramatic, or certainly were seen to be so at the time. The death of the Rev. Jackson near Pillar Rock in 1878 will be recounted below. In 1882 the Rev. J. Pope fell to his death on the Ennerdale face of Great Gable, and a further fatality occurred in 1883 - that of Walker on Pillar Rock, also to be mentioned below. Ten years later a university professor Milnes Marshall lost his life on Scafell. But the most serious accident of the early years was to take place on 21 September 1903, when R.W.Broadrick, an experienced climber, and three companions, fell to their deaths roped together on Scafell Pinnacle. It was timely, therefore, that the Fell and Rock Club addressed the problem, and gave it pride of place in its stated aims. A full list of the Club's objectives is given in the Appendix.

The anonymous chronicler of the founding of the Club is at pains to point out that he had discussed the formation of some such association with JWR himself 'well over a quarter of a century' earlier. He presents this as 'a plain statement of the facts surrounding the Club's formation', adding (and leaving an unwritten 'however' to be inferred by the reader) that 'it would be ungracious and unjust to withhold from Mr. Scantlebury and his indefatigable local committee the fullest measure of appreciation of their untiring efforts'. Is this perhaps the pen of the ubiquitous George Seatree concealed behind the anonymity?

This account of the birth of climbing in the Lake District, with its strong accent on social factors, has necessarily done less than justice to the cumulative story of how the routes on the various rock-climbing venues were conquered, and by whom. The reason has been to situate JWR in the context of his time. There is an abundant literature recounting in greater detail the history of climbing and giving details of the climbs themselves, and a slimmed down version is given in the *Note on Sources* at the end of this book. It would be fitting none the less to conclude by situating JWR's exploits very schematically within an overall periodisation of climbing from a technical point of view.

In their *A Short History of Lakeland Climbing*, H.M Kelly & J.H.Doughty distinguish four main phases in that history. The first, up to the year 1880, they term the 'easy way', when individual climbers, not yet attached to others by a rope, made their way up rocks as best they might, no matter what kind of technical problem presented itself. This was the period before Haskett-Smith appeared on the scene. The second, the decade of the 1880s, was the 'gully and chimney' period, when climbers worked within the clefts in the rock structure. Overlapping with this, from 1890 to 1905, came what they call the 'ridge and arête (or rib)' period, and finally, from 1905 to today, climbing in the Lakes entered on a 'slab and wall' period.

The names of the two latter periods speak for themselves. The next chapter will include examples drawn from the first period. It was, however, almost entirely in the second period that JWR's climbing activity took place.

A few remarks might be appropriate here on the use made of ropes in the early years of Lake District climbing. In a note in the Wasdale Head Hotel visitors' book, Haskett-Smith remarked that the use of ropes fell within a category of 'illegitimate means' of climbing. His diary from 1881 shows that others were then using ropes, but that he and his companions 'classed ropes with spikes and ladders, as a means by which bad climbers were enabled to go where none but the best climbers had any business to be'. On the other hand, there is a traditional belief that JWR was among the first to use the rope in his rock-climbing. Seatree made the remark that on one of his expeditions with JWR he was surprised to see that his companion had brought a rope with him. As late as in 1893, in an account of the ascent he made of Pillar's North Face with JWR, O.G.Jones wrote: 'Then a fifty-feet length of rope made its appearance; it had been hidden in a bag during our walk, lest we should alarm the folks at Gatesgarth'. But in fact for a long time — as far back at least as in the celebrated ascent of Pillar Rock in 1875 by the Reverend Jackson, to be recounted below — ropes had been used as a form of security by being suspended from a fixed point or dangled by a companion higher up the climb. The literature on the 1880s has many examples of this, and also of climbers swarming up ropes so attached. Photos from that decade show ropes being used in the way now standard, to attach a pair or a team of climbers to each other (though not yet to the rock by systematic and secure belaying), but the use of the rope followed so gradual and varied a course that no purpose is served by seeking to fix a definitive point for its birth as a climbing aid.

1 Marshall, J.D. and J.K.Walton, *The Lake Counties from 1830 to the Mid-Twentieth Century*, Manchester: Manchester University Press, 1981, p.191.

2 Brailsford, Dennis, *British Sport – A Social History*, Cambridge UK and Maryland MA: Lutterworth and Barnes & Noble, 1992

3 Lowerson, John, *Sport and the English Middle Classes, 1870-1914*, Manchester, New York : Manchester University Press, 1993.

4 Seatree, George, 'In Memoriam – John W. Robinson', *Fell and Rock Climbing Club Journal*, 1:1 (1907), pp. 6-7.

Chapter 3:
Pillar and Beyond

If you go from Wasdale Head up the Black Sail pass and fork left from its top to walk along the craggy flank of Pillar Mountain you will encounter Robinson's cairn, erected after JWR's death under Haskett-Smith's direction to commemorate the dalesman's association with Pillar Rock. You will in all likelihood already have been walking on the High Level route to the Rock which was pioneered by JWR himself. Affixed to the rock face close to the cairn you will find a tablet in JWR's honour, mounted in dramatic circumstances to be described in the final chapter. While the visitor-pioneers of rock-climbing in the Lakes introduced in the last chapter were strongly connected with Wasdale Head, it is with Pillar Rock that climbing history has associated JWR. From his first ascent of the Rock in 1882 JWR put a stamp on the Rock which has proved indelible. At the same time, this should not be allowed to diminish his prowess on other crags.

The historical significance of Pillar Rock is that it offered to the early adepts of the new sport a terrain admirably suited to that pursuit. No one goes to Pillar Rock except to engage in climbing crags, using both hands and feet. Indeed, the story of climbing on Pillar is a central part of the early development of rock-climbing itself condensed into one utterly rocky location. Moreover, the crag's detached character sets it apart from the two other prime venues for Lakeland's first climbers – the Napes face of Gable and Scafell Crag. With feeling born of experience, George Seatree asked:

> If a poll of Lakeland climbers were taken to ascertain their views as to the most interesting cluster of climbs in the district, would not there be a great preponderance in favour of the climbs of the Pillar Rock in Ennerdale? The vastness of the great buttress, the wonderful topography of the rock, the unsurpassed grandeur of its crag scenery, its unique situation overlooking Cumberland's wildest valley, threaded by the brawling Lisa, the immense variety of its courses, the splendid annals of the conquest of the severer climbs,

Pillar Rock's North Climb. the forbidding northern face of Pillar Rock was a magnet for the early Lakeland rock-climbers, offering a challenging variety of possible routes. The first ascent was made by Haskett-Smith with Geoffrey Hastings and Cecil Slingsby on 27th July, 1891. JWR made the second ascent in October, 1891, with Slingsby, following the same route.

and, alas, the tragic interest attached to others, all tend to accord it the foremost position among our local rock-climbing haunts.[1]

Pillar comes on the scene long before the birth of climbing with ropes. We saw that it got a mention in Wordsworth, anchoring the origin of the Pillar story in the works of the Romantic poets. Rock-climbers were tackling it long before the years when Haskett-Smith and his fellows were visiting Wasdale Head. To that extent the early ascents of Pillar constitute an *Ur*-history of Lakeland climbing.

It was not JWR who launched Pillar Rock into prominence among climbers. The work was done long before he made his first ascent of it. The person honoured by history as the first conqueror of Pillar Rock is John Atkinson, a shepherd who lived at Croftfoot, Ennerdale. On 25 July 1826 *The Cumberland Pacquet* reported that on July 9 Atkinson had scaled the Rock, succeeding where 'thousands' had so far failed. The interest of this surreal exaggeration is that this was clearly the moment when rock-climbing came to be viewed as business for newspaper reporting. When Wordsworth composed his poem *The Brothers* in 1800 he took it for granted that shepherds were familiar with the Rock. He describes it as rising '…like a column from the vale, Whence by our shepherds it is called THE PILLAR [his capitals]', and he talks of its 'aery summit crowned with heath'. Atkinson and the three other shepherds who hastened to repeat his climb in its immediate aftermath may indeed have been bemused to find greatness thus thrust upon them. History, however, was soon to eclipse the fact that it was the shepherds and the sheep of the fells who were at the forefront in the very earliest phase of Lakeland rock-climbing.

H.M.Kelly says of that first recorded ascent:

It cannot be gainsaid that in [this first ascent of Pillar Rock] was the first seed of what we know as English rock-climbing. The climbing of rocks as a sport in itself parted ways with mountaineering as then known, i.e. the attainment of the summit of a mountain by the least arduous route. True, there was no positive break from tradition: the change was more evolutionary, but one can see here the branch forking from the stem. Here was a definite attempt to get to a summit – not of a mountain, mark you! – by way of difficult rocks.2

It was some time before this seed sprouted and grew to maturity.

Pioneers of the Fell and Rock Climbing Club, including
E. H. P. Scantlebury and Alan Craig, who are credited with
being the moving figures in the founding of the Club.

This was 27 years before JWR was born, and a full 55 years before Haskett-Smith's first visit to Wasdale Head. By the time of the next recorded ascent, it was no longer shepherds who were shaping the annals of Pillar Rock, but visitors to the Lake District. In 1850 a naval lieutenant by the name of Wilson scaled it, as did the celebrated C.A.O. Baumgartner and two other climbers in the same year. Baumgartner's ascent is a landmark in itself. It was the first made by a cragsman, one of those who came to Lakeland specifically to climb rocks and who made names for themselves by long devotion to Lakeland climbing. Wilson contributed a minor landmark in leaving a bottle on the summit with his name in it. Adding names was to become an honoured practice. The first woman up was a Miss A.Barker of Gosforth in 1869. She was followed in 1873 by Mary 'May' Westmorland of Penrith, who climbed the Rock with her two brothers in 1873, and she in turn was followed by Ann Creer in 1875.

JWR was particularly appreciative of the contribution of Mary Westmorland and her brothers in making Pillar Rock so well known to climbers. 'People looked upon it as a terrible object until the Westmorlands had climbed the Rock and fully explained how the work could best be done', he commented later in a talk to the Penrith Literary Society in 1895. By the 1860s it was no longer simply a matter of reaching the summit of the Rock, but of pioneering differing routes up it. These, for climbers, constitute the juice of the history of Pillar Rock, but to give the full detail here would distort the broader purpose of this biography. Of more general interest is a table that George Seatree later drew up giving the number of ascents made between 1826 and 1875. It can only be taken as approximate, since he repeats the finishing year of each ten-year period as the first year of the next (see page 48).

In 1875 there enters into the record the remarkable figure of the Reverend James Jackson, mentioned above. This elderly Church of England clergyman had bought himself a house at Sandwith near St Bees. Questioning in the press whether Mary Westmorland had in fact reached the summit of Pillar, he was soon engaged in a vigorous dispute with Miss Westmorland's brothers, who offered to give him a message to put in the bottle on the summit if he cared to do the climb himself. Riled, 'Steeple' Jackson contacted George Seatree to tap his expertise and prepared to

Ascents of Pillar Rock, 1826 to 1875

Period	Number of ascents
1826 to 1850	6
1850 to 1866	22
1866 to 1873	31
1874	10
1875	50

Source: Seatree, George, 'Reminiscences of early Lakeland mountaineering', FRCCJ, 2:1 (1908), p.16 (dates of periods as given by Seatree).

tackle the Rock himself. Hankinson cites his words: 'If under your guidance I should succeed in reaching the top of the Rock you will have an opportunity of crowning me with parsley, fern or heather as "The Pedestrian Patriarch of the Pillarites" for in April 1875 I shall have entered my 80th year'. He did not undertake the ascent alone, but took with him a younger man, John Hodgson.

The summit-bottle duly received a pre-written card, declaring: 'The Patriarch of the Pillarites, born A.D. 1796. Ascended the Pillar Rock A.D. 1875'. He left a further bottle with a card written in Greek and, being given to composing doggerel verses, he added:

> If in your mind you will fix,
> When I make the Pillar my toy,
> I was born in 1, 7, 9, 6,
> And you'll think me a nimble old boy.

In the following year, 1876, Jackson made a further ascent of Pillar, this time alone but, as before with Hodgson, using ropes attached to spikes. Two years later, now at the age of 82, he set off to climb Pillar Rock again, but failed to return. His body was found near the base of the Rock – with another four lines of Jacksonian verse in his pocket prepared for the bottle.

It was four years after this that JWR entered the story of Pillar Rock, when he was 29 years old and had been running the family farm with his father for some years. His first ascent of the Rock took place on 28 June

The Rev. 'Steeple' James Jackson, the self-styled 'Patriarch of the Pillarites', who climbed Pillar Rock at the age of 79

1882 in the company of J.E.Walker, the headmaster of a Quaker school in Saffron Walden and himself descended from a long line of yeoman farmers in Loweswater. This was the year of Haskett-Smith's seminal second stay in Wasdale Head. He and JWR thus made their acquaintance with Pillar Rock at roughly the same time, and it was the start of two decades during which their partnership was to dominate climbing on it.

It might be asked why JWR is so firmly associated with Pillar in particular, given that he contributed to opening the major climbs on other fells as well, and that he was not involved in the earliest ascents of the Rock. One answer is simply that he devoted so much attention to it. By the time of his death in 1907 he had made 101 ascents. The camping trip that JWR made with Seatree in 1885 started and finished with climbs on the crag that was so dear to both of them. In his record of the trip JWR exults in having by then climbed the Pillar by eight distinct ways and two variations. Of especial significance was his finding and establishing the High Level route to it, but there are other answers that reveal aspects of his character that were to endear him to the entire climbing fraternity of his day. In particular, he was unsparing in the time and attention he was prepared to devote to others, and this included helping people, young and old, in making their own ascents. 'He was never happier,' writes Seatree, 'than when engaged in bringing strangers and novices to his favourite shrine, the Ennerdale Pillar Rock. No effort and no sacrifice were too great for him to make in order to reach a given rendezvous to aid those who desired his trusty leadership'.[3]

It is clear that he was proud of this. His diary contains a list of the people with whom he had climbed Pillar Rock. It bears the names of many for whom he was clearly acting as guide and tutor, but many of the great figures in the history of Lakeland climbing at the time are also mentioned: Charles Hopkinson, O.G.Jones, Cecil Slingsby, C.A.O. Baumgartner, George Seatree, Geoffrey Hastings, Frederick Bowring and, of course, Haskett-Smith. The names of a total of 92 people are given, with a note that many of them climbed the Pillar with JWR a number of times.

Recollections of JWR published even after his death dwell on his role as a guide on Pillar Rock, such as an article on him in the *Fell and Rock Climbing Club Journal* in 1946 by an anonymous 'Founder Member' who had been piloted up the Rock together with a Miss

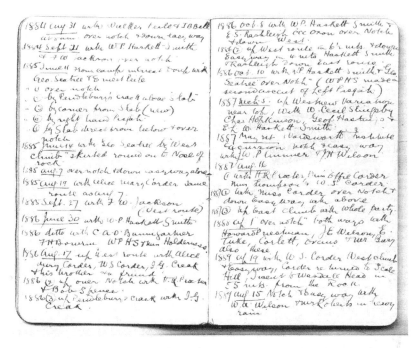

Two pages of JWR's Diary, recording climbs on Pillar Rock.

Crompton of the Manchester University Settlement and Lawrence Scott, the younger son of the editor of the *Manchester Guardian*. More substantial is Owen Glynne Jones's account of his ascent with JWR of the North Face in 1893. This appears in Jones's *Rock-Climbing in the English Lake District*, and is one of the best extended descriptions of a major climb performed under JWR's guidance, characteristically 'with the occasional anecdote thrown in'.

So much time spent on the Rock with others naturally increased the possibility of mishaps. JWR himself on one occasion suffered an accident that could have resulted in his own death and that of others roped to him. He was climbing on the inhospitable north face of the Rock with Geoffrey Hastings and Norman Collie, and attempting the hand traverse on it. As Collie told the story:

> The day was bitterly cold and Robinson was a short distance from the traverse. His hands were so frozen that he could not hold on or get back. He called out,

51

Moss Ghyll on the central face of Scafell Crag was first conquered on Boxing Day, 1892, by Norman Collie, Geoffrey Hastings and JWR. This was the occasion when Norman Collie defied accepted norms by chipping a foothold in the rock, with Hastings' ice-axe.The resulting foothold has since been known as "Collie's Step". The leading climber in the photograph is resting his right foot on it.

'I can't hold on any longer', and then fell straight onto the ledge below, bounded out into the air, turning a somersault backwards, and pitching onto a great projection some 30 feet lower down, hitting it with his shoulder. At the exact moment that he hit the grass, the strain came on the rope. If this had not happened, nothing would have stopped him, and the whole party would have been dragged after him. Sheer luck had saved us all.4

This emphasis on the particular association of JWR with Pillar Rock follows the legend that has grown up around him, but it should not be allowed to diminish his achievements elsewhere in the Lake District. The most notable cases are those where he was involved in pioneering new climbs. It is a reflection on JWR's whole attitude to mountaineering, however, and to the element of competition inherent in it, that in opening up routes he was almost without exception acting as a member of a team.

A celebrated example of this teamwork was the conquering of Moss Ghyll, the only one of the three great gullies on the central face of Scafell Crag that had not been climbed when Geoffrey Hastings, Norman Collie and JWR addressed the task on Boxing Day, 1892. The outing was to have a great resonance in the history of climbing through what has come to be known as 'Collie's step' when that distinguished mountaineer committed the heinous – to climbers – crime of making a hold by attacking the rock with an ice-axe. A great boulder, overhanging the route high in the gully, had barred the way and impeded the ascent. A route that would circumvent it was found, but there were no handholds at all, and Collie's first attempt at securing a foothold almost ended in disaster. Hankinson quotes Collie in *The Scottish Mountaineering Journal:* 'What followed I have no doubt will be severely criticised by more orthodox mountaineers than ourselves ... [with Hastings's ice axe] *I hacked a step in the rock*'.

One of JWR's greatest days was 20 September 1884 when he and Haskett-Smith, in thick mist and rain, achieved the first climb of Scafell Pinnacle (then known as Deep Ghyll Pillar) by Steep Ghyll from Rake's Progress. This was to be one of his favourite climbs. He was to make 50 ascents of 'DGP', the fiftieth being the last rock climb he made, one year before his death. Other first ascents in which he participated included that of Black Chimney and Green Crag in the Buttermere

JWR leads W.Blunt and V.Blake on an ascent of Scafell Pinnacle. They are roped to each other, but the need to belay climbers to the rock had not yet become standard practice.

valley, and the Iron Crag Chimney, near Southwaite Ghyll, which he conquered with F.W.Jackson and the Abraham brothers in June 1896. In September 1893 O.G.Jones, with JWR and, in Hankinson's words, 'under his guidance', made the first ascent of Sergeant Crag Gully and opened up some other gully climbs on the flank of High Stile, overlooking Buttermere. JWR's outings with Haskett-Smith resulted in many first ascents as a pair, such as their opening up of Dow Crag, but the partnership was so close and they climbed together so frequently that they created many new routes that today go under names given them by subsequent climbers.

We have an account of one of the more alarming moments of JWR's climbing career written in his own hand. It occurs in his article 'Camping among the crags' and illustrates his characteristic concern for the safety of others. The occasion was an ascent of the Mickledore Chimney when JWR and Seatree were climbing in a group of five, which included Frederick Bowring and Ernest Piele, a young friend of the Robinson family, for whom JWR accordingly felt responsible. Bowring and Piele had climbed up Broad Stand, to one side of the chimney and outside it, while JWR, Seatree and the fifth member of the group were engaged in the difficult climb inside it. JWR recounts how he heard a deafening roar and saw masses of stones falling down the chimney above him.

I cried 'Look out! And ducked under a crag with my face turned towards the edge above me over which it must have come. I could not see the other two, they got a little higher towards the great over-hanging rock. Those were awful moments; Seatree says he hopes never to go through such again... The next moment a great stone about 18 inches square came bounding over, dancing from side to side as it came down and making great stars on the sides of the chimney where it struck. It was followed by a great fall of fragments of every size and shape across the entire chimney, more or less, and the air seemed darkened for a few moments. I jumped up and said are you hurt? No, Mr. Bowring are you there? Yes. 'We are all right.' Who set it off? 'Piele; he is in the Chimney above.' What did he go up there for?

The unfortunate – and less than conscientious – Piele had left Broad Stand and entered the chimney.

Many of the ascents recorded in JWR's diary did not involve rock-climbing at all, but were made on standard walkers' tracks. The diary is, in fact, largely an enumeration of summits reached, and presents to us a fellsman for whom climbing on rocks was an extension, if a novel and exhilarating one, of an established habit of simply walking on the fells. He tells us that in addition to his hundred and one climbing ascents of Pillar Rock between 1882 and 1906, he scaled Scafell Pinnacle over 50 times between 1884 and 1906. On standard tracks he went up Great Gable 33 times between 1877 and 1903. He climbed Great End 19 times, Scafell itself 55 times, Scafell Pikes and Pillar Mountain 32 and 30 times respectively. The earliest ascents actually mentioned in the diary are of these two latter summits in 1874, the year in which he met Seatree, and the one that we must take as the start of his recorded climbing career. Helvellyn he climbed only five times, while his four ascents of Skiddaw suggest that the walk was found as tedious a century ago as it usually is today

JWR's great familiarity with his native fells was frequently remarked on by his climbing colleagues. Collie remarked that 'Robinson is *the* great authority on the hills of the Lake District. There is not a rock on a mountainside that he does not know. In sunshine or mist, in daytime or at midnight, he will guide one safely over passes or down precipitous mountainsides. Every tree and every stone is a landmark to him'.[5]

Nowhere is JWR's enjoyment in going along as well as up more evident than in his participation in an informal competition that developed in the 1880s and 90s to see how many summits could be reached within 24 hours.

According to JWR's *Scrapbook* the fashion seems to have been set some time around 1850 by a T. M. Elliott of Trinity College Cambridge. The start was a modest one, taking in only a series of peaks in one particular direction from Wasdale Head: Great Gable, Kirkfell, Pillar Mountain, Steeple, Red Pike and Yewbarrow, covering some 15 miles in eight and a half hours. Some dozen years after him 'an Alpine climber', with the Langdale guide Mackereth, covered a wider range – Scafell Pike, Bow Fell, Helvellyn, Skiddaw in a single day. This exploit was followed by that of Henry Irvine Jenkinson on 17 June 1876, who included Gable and Saddleback and turned in a time of 23 hours, covering some 45 miles.

But it was Arthur Tucker (later to become a bishop) with his three brothers, who in June 1878 really laid down the challenge. Leaving Elterwater at four in the morning they took in Bow Fell, Scafell Pike, Skiddaw, Saddleback and Helvellyn, arriving back at eleven at night. The distance was reckoned to be over 50 miles, but contained a good deal of road walking. Great Gable was not included.

At some point after the Tuckers' expedition Charles Pilkington and his cousins covered the same peaks, with Great End in addition, but they set off in thick mist and they had taken 24 hours and 25 minutes when they arrived back at their starting point at Lodore.

It was the time taken and the distance covered by the Tuckers that were the targets taken by JWR when he planned the walk that he himself accomplished in October 1893. He also had the walks of Pilkington and Jenkinson in mind. 'Some people tell me that Pilkington's walk has never been beaten but I fancy he is behind the Tuckers', he wrote in a letter of 9 November 1892 to A.W.Rumney, who had been suggested to him as a possible companion for the walk, and he asked Rumney to tell him 'what the late Mr Jenkinson did. I cannot find out'.

In the letter he is at pains to disassociate himself from the 'record breakers'. This is, in fact, one of the many cases where JWR's undoubted modesty conflicts with an equally clear wish to acquire merit through exploits on the fells. Even if he was merely measuring himself against his own capacities, it was difficult for him not to be drawn into competitive situations, particularly when, as here, others clearly saw themselves as competing against each other. He writes to Rumney that he did not take time to explain his intentions fully,

and therefore I am not surprised that you regard my object as being Record Breaking. I could never hope to break Tuckers' if I wanted to, but all the same I am interested in finding out what others have done. People say 'Why go at all, you of all people, who have always condemned people for doing too much in one day?' This is perfectly true: I have said it many a time, but somehow during the last two years the idea has got into my head of seeing how many mountains I can do in a day. I am slow and should never dream of cutting or attempting a record but, you will excuse my saying so, I have always felt that if I could get or had any slight advantage over some others it was merely knowing the Scawfell Range pretty well and for that reason I intend to put in Scawfell itself, which has always been left out as being out of the way and cut off by Mickledore.

He adds that, should he and Rumney fail to match the Tuckers' exploit and do a walk on a smaller scale, 'it will be solely for our pleasure'.

A second letter, written probably within a few days of the first, makes it clear that the walk was not to be seen entirely as a competitive venture. 'My present idea is, if there is very fine weather *next* full moon and not too hard frost, to have a start for the fun of the thing and, if I don't get all round or in very poor time, have another walk in the spring'. He then presents his proposed route, to take in nine peaks in 20 hours and 30 minutes. 'If I do these nine mountains in a day, plenty of people will say it was never done as they tell me now of Jenkinson, but that is not the point, I do it for my own pleasure. Now if when the time comes you care to start with me I shall be delighted to have you, it will be fun amongst those high mountains.' With his usual care to avoid drawing inexperienced people into danger, he asks Rumney not to pass details of his planned route 'to any of those rash youths you speak of'.

In the end it was not with Rumney that JWR carried out the walk but with a certain G.B.Gibbs. They started from Keswick, in appalling weather which promised to make the walk problematical from the start. They set off, none the less, down Borrowdale to climb Great Gable (presumably via Sty Head Pass). From there they took in Scafell (by Pike's Traverse from Skew Gill and Deep Gill, and the West Wall Traverse), and proceeded via Broad Stand to Scafell Pikes. According to a later account in the *Yorkshire Post* the going was already difficult because of the ice and the wind-driven snow.[6] They had no rope or axe, and had to improvise by using a rucksack, 'Mr Gibbs holding one strap while Mr Robinson hung hold of the other and kicked the ice off the ledges'. From there to Great End, Bowfell, Langdale, Combe Head and Wythburn and onto Helvellyn, still in a blizzard. When they got to Threlkeld after taking in Saddleback, Skiddaw seemed well within their grasp. Once engaged on that long and exposed climb, however, they encountered a strong headwind, and the weather had become so atrocious that the walk had to be abandoned. The time taken by then was 23 hours and 25 minutes.[7] It is to be noted that this was October. All the other participants in the informal competition had chosen to do their walk in

The Great Pitch, Sergeant Crag gully.
JWR made the first ascent of Sergeant Crag gully with O.G.Jones on
6th September, 1893.

June, July or August. Although JWR and Gibbs accomplished less than they had intended, their walk has ever since commanded a great deal of respect. Also, whilst they did not in the end take in Skiddaw (nor Pillar, which few of the competitors included), they climbed both Scafell Pikes and Scafell itself, which meant dealing with Mickledore, and in thoroughly nasty weather.

The competition was to continue thereafter. In his *The First Tigers,* Alan Hankinson relates how in September 1902 R.W.Broadrick and a Mr Dawson of Sale covered seventy miles, with 18,500 feet of ascent, in just under the 24 hours, taking in Pillar Mountain, Scafell Pikes, Great End, Bow Fell, Helvellyn, Saddleback and Skiddaw. In 1904 R.W.Wakefield was to walk 74 miles (64 by the map), with 16,000 feet of ascent, in 19 hours 53 minutes, including stops for food. By then, however, developments in mountaineering (and fell-running) equipment and clothing had transformed the character of the competition.

As concerns less competitive walks and climbs, calculations by Richard Hall based on JWR's diary reveal that the month of the year in which he climbed most was August (77 ascents), then September with 56, and June with 52. No ascents are recorded in February and only one in November. The full list is:

January	19	February	-	March	21	April	35
May	11	June	52	July	10	August	77
September	56	October	27	November	-	December	16

There were also 23 ascents with no date given. Over the 24 years 1882 to 1906 this averages a little over one per month (but three in the Augusts and more than two in the Septembers). This must seem little to today's visitors to the Lake District, who might expect to average a peak a day over a fortnight's holiday. But, first, the fact that Blencathra gets no mention in JWR's listing of his ascents suggests that his figures are incomplete, since we know that he was familiar with this peak. Second, JWR was not a holiday visitor. He had a farm to manage, and the low figure for July is no doubt to be accounted for by the need to attend to the harvest and other pressing summer priorities. While JWR looms large in the history of rock-climbing, this should not lead us to overestimate the time he devoted to that activity. Part of the aim of this book is to set his climbing record in the context of the busy life of a farmer, with substantial commitments in local administrative affairs.

His climbing diary deals with more than the ascents that he made. It reveals a love of nature which greatly impressed his fellow climbers, and which he inherited from his father. The diary opens, in fact, with some notes of natural history – sightings of rare birds (a ring-ouzel, for instance) and the discovery of some less accessible nests (of a buzzard, and a peregrine falcon). But what captures the imagination more than the record of the peaks that he climbed is his routine trudges from his home in Lorton down the length of Lorton Vale and over Scarth Gap to join his climbing colleagues on Pillar Rock, leaving before the dawn and returning in the evening, the glim of his lantern visible to the Nelsons at Gatesgarth as he came down the pass.[8]

JWR showed no great enthusiasm for mountaineering abroad. Seatree informs us that his friend made his acquaintance with the Alps in 1898, climbing several peaks, but mere acquaintance it remained and he made no further visits there.[9] According to Bill Birkett he 'accompanied Collie in the Himalayas', but this is almost certainly apocryphal. There are no other references to what would have been an extravagant excursion for a Lakeland farmer. On the other hand his papers contain a collection of press cuttings that reveal an interest in the exploits of others not only in the Lake District but also in Wales, the Alps and the Himalayas. The clippings were obviously chosen chiefly for their dramatic interest, since the majority concern mountaineering accidents.

Pillar Rock, then, was but one destination in JWR's repertoire of walks and climbs, even though it is with that crag that his name is most associated in the annals of climbing in the Lake District.

This chapter has concentrated on JWR's achievements on the rocks. Some inkling of what JWR was like as a person has necessarily shown through. The more detailed portrait of his character which follows will provide a perspective on a man whom the early climbing fraternity in the Lake District regarded with such respect, and with no little affection.

1 Seatree, George, 'Reminiscences of early Lakeland mountaineering', *Fell and Rock Climbing Club Journal*, 2:11, pp.13-14.
2 Kelly, H.M., 'Pillar Rock and neighbouring climbs', *Fell and Rock Climbing Club*

Journal, 6:2, pp.131-2.

3 Seatree, George, 'In memoriam – John Wilson Robinson', *Fell and Rock Climbing Club Journal*, 1:1, 1907, p.7.

4 Hankinson, *The First Tigers*, Bassenthwaite: Melbeck, 1972, p.92-3, citing *The Scottish Mountaineering Club Journal*.

5 *Penrith Observer*, 10 December 1895, reporting on a talk by JWR to the Penrith Literary Society. JWR's Scrapbook.p.71.

6 'Mountaineering in Cumbria: The gentle art of peak-bagging', 18 January 1906, *JWR's Scrapbook*, p.61.

7 Lefebure, Molly, *The English Lakes*, Batsford, 1964, pp.157/8, drawing on M.J.Baddeley, *Guide to the Lake District*, London: Ward, Locke and Co Ltd.. 1980.

8 Acording to Seatree, 'In memoriam...', *Fell and Rock Climbing Club Journal*, 1:1, 1907, p.7; Griffin has him leaving the house at three - A.H.Griffin, *Inside the Real Lakeland*, pp.59-60)

9 Seatree, 'In memoriam...', p.8; also Alan Hankinson, *A Century on the Crags: the story of rock-climbing in the Lake District*, London: Dent, 1988, p.31.

Chapter 4:
JWR — A Portrait

What was he like as a person, this Quaker dalesman and climbing pioneer? In his physical appearance, the descriptions we have of JWR show a tall and well-built man, with merry blue eyes, sandy-coloured hair and bushy side-whiskers reaching under a firm chin that was kept shaven (see Frontispiece). When walking and climbing he is said to have habitually worn a Norfolk jacket of yellowish brown Harris tweed, with twill knee-breeches, brown stockings and boots said by a memorialist to have been the work of a local cobbler (the 'Harris tweed' of the record is equally likely to have been of more local origin). Some photos show him wearing a cap, others a high-crowned hat, others again a deerstalker, but all accounts agree that under whatever headgear his head was bald and shiny.

As to his character, his many companions on the rocks were universal in their appreciation of his sociability, his wisdom, his generous concern for others, and the way in which his climbing activities grew out of an organic love of nature and the fells. 'What amazed me about John', wrote an anonymous 'Founder Member' in the *Fell and Rock Climbing Club Journal*, 'was that in spite of all his business cares ... he contrived to oblige the numberless people anxious to walk and climb with him. Never was there such a friendly man. Never was there so companionable a man. He paid dearly for his ready response to the importunities of visitors to the Lake District. Often he used to work through the night that the work of the day should not be put off to the morrow'.

These personal characteristics seem to have been as much valued as his exploits on the rocks. True, his premature death at the very moment when the Fell and Rock Climbing Club was being formed understandingly generated particular expressions of praise, but there can be no doubt about their sincerity. The record of his private life offers a more rounded picture, though such personal failings as he had do not bring into question the legend that grew up around his life as a cragsman. His response to the tribulations that life imposed on him at home we leave for a later chapter.

Kern Knotts Chimney
The first ascent of the chimney was made on 26th December, 1893, by
JWR, O.G.Jones and W.Fowler in heavy rain. JWR ("Nestor")
provided Jones with a shoulder to step on.

Kern Knotts Crack
Later that day this was the scene of a celebrated spat between
O.G.Jones and JWR, when Jones eyed the crack with a view to notching
up a first ascent. Jones's approach to rock-climbing was audacious to
the point, often, of rashness. while JWR tended to decry exploits that
might draw inexperienced climbers into taking totally unnecessary
risks. "Nestor, with his characteristic caution", Jones wrote much later,
"vetoed the whole affair and vowed he would never speak to me again
if I attempted to climb it".

In this one it is the image of 'John', and the impression that he made on others, that will concern us.

It is difficult to view in separation JWR's sociability, his wisdom and his generous concern for others, since each is a particular aspect of the complete personality. They add up to an image of JWR as a great communicator and an instinctive educator. These qualities are not frequently encountered in the great figures of rock climbing, and it is partly for this reason that JWR stands out in the sport's early history.

The way in which JWR took others with him in his enthusiasm for scaling rocks has already been noted. He was always willing to give time, attention and encouragement to others, particularly to young people and those making their first acquaintance with the rocks. It was also seen above that many first ascents recorded by others were made with JWR's support and under his guidance. He made no discrimination between the sexes in this. 'A true ladies' man was our dear old friend in the best sense of the word', Cecil Slingsby said of him, 'and many a winsome lassie had he introduced to the heart of the fells and to the best climbs in Lakeland'.[1] JWR himself took a rather more prosaic view of what he was doing. In an article in the *West Cumberland Times* of 8 March 1890, he lamented that 'some people fall into the error of underrating a climb simply because a lady, to use their own expression, has been "hauled up"'. George Seatree, for his part, saw no reason to make any distinction in JWR's attitude to the sexes: 'J.W.R.'s diary tabulates between 30 and 40 ladies who have been under his kindly escort to the summit of Pillar Rock, and the roll of the sterner sex he has led and helped up there, on to Scawfell Pinnacle, and the climbs of Great Gable must be legion. He was never happier than when engaged in bringing strangers and novices to his favourite shrine, the Ennerdale Pillar Rock'.[2]

Part of the skill of the true educator lies in enabling people to appropriate what they have learned, by leading them to feel that they have been doing the discovering for themselves. It is a capacity that JWR appears to have had in abundance. It was acknowledged by, among others, his partner on the rocks Haskett-Smith, with the words, 'Never was there a man more utterly unselfish, never one who so cleverly continued to give the impression that he and not you was the person benefited'.[3]

This attention to the needs and interests of others was matched by his concern over climbing accidents. The scrapbook of press cuttings which he kept on mountaineering at home and abroad was chiefly concerned with them. His papers also contain a smaller book of press cuttings of a more general kind (letters from the *Whitehaven News* about Pillar, articles on Lakeland from *The Graphic* magazine, two accounts of crossing the Sty Head and Black Sail passes in the dark), but George Bott has pointed out the frequency even in these general items of headings such as 'The Shocking Accident on Great Gable', 'The Terrible Death on the Cumberland Hills', 'The Alpine Death-Roll', and 'Fearful Fall on the Ennerdale Fells'. JWR was always aware of the dangers of climbing, and preferred not to push those whom he was helping beyond their capacities. Richard Hall recalls how on one occasion JWR set out with him and Richard's brother to climb Pillar. On the way to the Rock 'J.W.R. kept looking anxiously at the snow-capped misty hills...The climb that day saw us no further than the top of the West Scree at the foot of which John roped us together. "By thunder but it looks bad," said he, so my brother recollects, whilst I remember his saying, "We won't go on, it was like this when poor Walker went over Walker's Gully"'. The reference here is to an event in the winter of 1883 when a young man of 17 named Walker who was on Pillar Rock answered a call for help from two climbers below. In an attempt to glissade down on the snow he overshot them and fell over a precipice to his death.

It was Owen Glynne Jones who applied the nick-name 'Nestor' to JWR in view of his wisdom and experience, in a reference to Agamemnon's loyal counsellor in the *Iliad*, the 'King of Sandy Pylos'. He cites an occasion in 1896 when JWR met up with him and the Abraham brothers, George and Ashley, on Sty Head Pass and the party inspected the still unclimbed Kern Knotts. JWR argued against making the tricky ascent on the grounds that it might lead to other, less skilful climbers taking risks and courting disaster. Jones, whose formidable bravery on the rocks was seen by many as close to bravado, disagreed. Hankinson records JWR's parting words as he turned back down to Borrowdale: 'Well, Jones,... if you climb that crack, I'll never speak to you again'.

JWR's aversion to taking unnecessary risks was illustrated on another occasion, again involving O.G.Jones, recorded by Aleister

Crowley, a controversial climber who was to become celebrated as an advocate and practitioner of black magic. In his *Confessions,* Crowley relates how, on a holiday in Langdale in 1893,

I started to climb Scafell, chiefly with the idea of tackling some of the gullies which I had noticed on the great cliff. I had reached the grass traverse when I heard voices in the mist above me, and a few minutes later a powerful man with red whiskers and a rope about his shoulders came towards me from the cliff. It was J.W.Robinson, a local farmer who had laid the foundation of Cumberland climbing. He offered to show me some of the easier climbs. He had started that morning with a man named Owen Glynne Jones. Jones had insisted on trying to climb Steep Ghyll, which is for the most part a shallow gully of smooth slabs set at a dangerous angle. There is no reliable hold for hand or foot on the main pitch, which is some 80 feet high. As torrents of icy water were pouring off the crags, it was sheer foolhardiness to attempt it. Robinson had refused to do so, whereupon Jones had quarrelled with him and they had parted.

In the speech that he made when unveiling the plaque mounted in JWR's memory shortly after his death Cecil Slingsby emphasised this aspect of Robinson's personality: 'He was as bold as a lion but took no unwarrantable risks as he possessed the great moral courage of being able to sound a retreat when experience dictated that to advance would be to court danger'. In 1885, during JWR's celebrated camping holiday with George Seatree, we have him refusing to let Ernest Piele of Workington conclude a climb on Scafell with a team of more experienced climbers 'because he felt responsible for his safety'.

On another occasion he forbade the same Ernest Peile to join a party tackling the 'North Climb' on Scafell because he had no nails in his boots. It will be recalled that the Peile family was close to JWR, and this was not the only occasion when JWR intervened to protect Ernest from trouble. It was none the less characteristic of JWR's unwillingness to lead others into positions of danger, and Ernest Peile was by no means the only climber who benefited from JWR's caring attitude towards others.

Finally, on a celebrated occasion in 1906 JWR wrote to the *Manchester Guardian* taking Fred Botterill to task (erroneously according to Botterill) for recording in the press his success in making the first ascent of the north-west route up Pillar Rock. 'I do think it is full time', he wrote, 'that a word of warning went forth against the practice which I fear is becoming too common of drawing public attention to climbs of this kind until they have been well tried and proved to be safe'.

Mountaineering is a competitive sport, at a basic level as a means of testing one's own capacities of endurance, but it is competitive also in that it has involved a wish to be the first to conquer a peak or, in the specific case of rock climbing, pioneer a new route up a crag. When JWR was forming his climbing partnership with Haskett-Smith the search was on for new routes on rocks that until then had had no human hand or foot placed on them, and there was a natural tendency for climbers to wish to be the first up. Yet JWR's lack of jealousy of others is frequently mentioned in the memoirs of those who climbed with him. According to Richard Hall, C.A.O. Baumgartner wrote in a letter to Frederick Bowring, 'What I most admire about J.W.R. is his entire freedom from any jealousy of rival climbers'. This noted lack of jealousy, however, was combined with what might be termed a humble competitive streak, which came out in many of his remarks and notes. He described the brief article 'A Novice in the Snow', which he contributed to the first issue of the *Fell and Rock Climbing Club Journal*, as 'a description of bad mountaineering' – adding that 'it may warn someone not to do likewise'. This low-key competitiveness revealed itself also in occasional throw-away comments, as when during his camping holiday with George Seatree in 1885 the sight of two bell tents near the top of Red Pike above where the pair had pitched their own tents led JWR to remark 'I hope it'll be windy for their impudence [in] getting higher than we are'.

His humility, often commented upon, seems to have acted as a constraint on such competitive instincts as he had. Was it a case of a naturally competitive person being held in check by his Quaker values? There are recorded remarks and occasions that reveal a taste for teasing deriving apparently from an awareness of his own talent qualified by a reluctance to exploit it too much to the discomfort of others. It was an aspect of JWR's character that his close friend George Seatree described as 'his sly alertness in pouncing upon and turning to account, in happy vein, the humorous side of men and things as they came his way'.[4] One novice who was climbing with JWR and others on Pillar Rock describes how, having been on the end of the rope on the way up, he was alarmed to be invited to be the first to go down. When he hesitated JWR accommodatingly said that if he wanted he could be the last to leave. Only when one of the more accomplished climbers stepped forward to be the first away did it dawn on the novice that as the last one down he would have no supporting rope from above.

Despite all the provisos and qualifications, there is no doubt that JWR was subject to competitive feelings, even if he hedged them about when talking about them, as if he believed that there was something reprehensible in being competitive, which was probably the case. His comments to A.W.Rumney on the subject of the marathon walk that he was projecting will be recalled: 'I could never break Tucker's [record] if I wanted to, but all the same I am interested in what others have done'. The point is that Tucker, Jenkinson and JWR were each participating in the linear evolution of sport, with all the accompanying notions of recording achievement, whatever their subjective feelings on the matter were. They were *performing*, within a particular context provided by the unfolding history of sport. Rumney himself tells us that he refrained from acting as a pacemaker for JWR on the walk, fearing that at 40 years of age JWR might do himself an injury – 'for in spite of his protestations, it was an attempt at a record'.

Numerous accounts emphasise JWR's exuberance and cheerfulness. 'John smiled through life', wrote a 'founder member' of the Fell and Rock Climbing Club in an appreciation of JWR after his death. Richard Hall, who a generation later set down his recollection of JWR as a friend of his family, wrote: 'The question is, why was 'J.W.R.' so beloved? He was more than merely 'popular'. Why is it that his name, that so ordinary surname, mentioned among climbers who have known him brings such a whirl of recollections, tough climbs, jokes, fell walks before them *and something else too?'* Hall recalls how, in his Quaker family home:

There would be a hum of conversation and, the door opening, Friends would stop talking and see who entered, and most would give a smile of welcome when in would come, with smiling tanned face, sandy side whiskers, a bald head, a suit of good homespun tweed (such as Harris tweed), generally, too, of a sandy shade, matching the colour scheme of the person himself — and this was no other than John Wilson Robinson, yeoman and pioneer rock climber of Whinfell Hall. To me, a boy of 7, his advent was ever welcomed for he had a charm and fascination which was not created solely by his promise of a rare "three cornered Cape of Good Hope stamp" or the gift of several stuffed birds - but it was a natural attraction to a strong personality, who had mixed with many people beyond the usual circle of Cockermouth Friends - professors and college men - and who had himself moved among the silent hills and imbibed something of their strength, dignity and charm. After shaking hands all round, John would sink into a chair near a good listener and begin to talk. A favourite opening was "Did I tell you that story of how Professor Hopkinson and I &c &c...". It was generally a professor, though the name of W. P. Haskett Smith, Owen Glynne Jones, Mr Bowring, Cecil Slingsby, Alfred Rawlings, Major Cundhill, Geo Seatree, C.A.O. Baumgartner, Spences, Proctors, Corders, Wilberforce might come in equally well. But Drs were almost as common: Dr Norman Collie, Dr Wellford, Dr Gill, Dr Claude Wilson, not to forget Geoffrey Hastings. John must have met a great many professors: Profs Oliver and Bower, Prof. Weiss, Prof. Adamson were some of them. John would tell of some new ascent, describe the perilous passage of some great ice pitch or tell over some joke fresh from a professor staying at Wasdale Head.

From this it is clear that part of JWR's extreme sociability was his remarkable skill as a communicator. This was shown not only in his willingness to bring others to share his enthusiasm for the rocks, where communication became really a matter of education. It was shown also, and most remarkably, in his anecdotal skills. The climbing literature is full of references to JWR's talent as a raconteur. As a dalesman he had a good deal to tell the visitors who were his climbing companions about life in the Lake District and they were willing listeners.

JWR did not leave much for posterity in written form. Fortunately one of his rare writings illustrates well his penchant for a good story by including an example. This is the article that JWR contributed to an early issue of the *Fell and Rock Climbing Club Journal* entitled 'A novice in the snow'. Mainly about a climbing expedition on which he and his companion encountered the dangers of climbing in severe snow conditions, the article ends with one of JWR's yarns, as if that was his preferred and natural mode of communication, though in fact the entire article is written in his yarning style. The expedition in the snow was rounded off by the party's going to church on the Sunday morning, where it was welcomed with open arms by the vicar who regaled it with stories of dalesmen, 'in return for which', writes our own dalesman, 'perhaps I may be allowed to relate one or two of the vicar'. The following paragraph is worth reproducing in full, since it gives the flavour of JWR's yarns.

Do you see those walls on the fell sides?' he said, 'they were built by the ancient Britons when they fled from the Emperor Diocletian. Shades of the Romans, what antiquity! And the Herdwick sheep-farmers have kept them in repair ever since!' On another occasion, amongst the congregation numbering half-a-dozen, two Oxford dons were quietly seated. The Rev. gentleman did not know this and was quite ordinary in his sermon, but the following Sunday he was ready for them, and turning to the few dalesmen he said, 'Some of you, my people, will not, I fear, understand much of my discourse this morning, but, thank God, there are those present who will,' and off he plunged into the Greek Testament. The Dons could make nothing of it, until one of them, pulling out his own Greek Testament and looking up the passage, discovered that the preacher had turned over two pages.

Owen Glynne Jones, in his *Rock Climbing in the English Lake District,* recalls a case when JWR's energy mingled with his habitual yarning. He was with a party led by JWR and which was returning from Pillar Rock towards Scarth Gap at a forced pace set by their untiring leader. 'Luckily for his followers, the name of this pass, which is sometimes called Scarf Gap, reminded him of a very good story concerning another climber who went to an evening party without a dress tie.' The pause while the yarn was told enabled the party to recover its breath sufficiently to continue its journey to Buttermere.

Haskett-Smith tells how a young stranger who 'showed an intelligent interest in climbing' asked JWR if he knew where Doe Crags were. JWR said he did. 'Have you seen them?' asked the youth. 'Not properly' said Robinson. Later in the conversation the young man discovered that in fact Robinson was perfectly familiar with the Crags. When he was taken to task for claiming not to have seen them Robinson replied that he had been telling the truth. He and Haskett-Smith had often been there, 'but we have only *climbed* the rocks; we have never seen them yet'. Haskett-Smith says that it was one of Robinson's favourite yarns, though others may judge that it was not one of his best.[5]

JWR's own talks to public audiences offered a tempting platform for his yarns. Addressing the Penrith Literary Society in December 1895, he referred to the 'belief among farmers that stones *grew*'. One Borrowdale farmer had said to him, with reference to the enormous glacial boulder that stands in that valley, that he 'ken't t'Bowder Stone when it was t'size of a shoe'.

* * *

JWR's death led to a surge of appreciation within an already existing affection for him. Was this purely and simply appreciation of a climbing colleague? The question must be asked whether the appreciation stemmed not only from JWR's having been one of their number, and a highly successful one on the rocks, while at the same time being different from them as a native Lakelander. The more eminent JWR became on the rocks, the more marked became the difference, as perceived by the visiting climbers at Wasdale Head.

Another question must then be asked - was there a sense of awkwardness on the part of the 'off-comers' that they and JWR were equal on the rocks, but that he held, as it were, the philosopher's stone? He, a dalesman, could take to climbing on his familiar rocks; they, the visitors, could climb the rocks but could not become Lakelanders. Was there an element of *surprise* that the dalesman could be so clubbable, and did that surprise add to their bemused admiration? It is as if the Oxbridge academics felt that they were gaining a certain added credibility from their association with the dalesman, which boosted the eminence that they accorded him.

While his climbing partnership with Haskett-Smith is the most obvious of his claims to fame, it was JWR's personality, together with the knowledge of the fells that he derived from his life as a dalesman, that has had the greatest influence in placing him in the pantheon of English rock-climbing. In A.H.Griffin's words, 'Robinson's name will live in mountain circles, not so much because he was a great climber or walker, but rather because he was such a lovable man and because to him there was no place like the Lakeland fells'.

In the second part of this book we move away from the climbing legend to look at the life that lay behind JWR's motivations and shaped his behaviour and attitudes. The sources now change, and values that are subliminal in the climbing account emerge in a clearer light. The background, too, changes; from having set JWR's life in the context of the birth of a new sport we now have to set it in other social aspects of Lake District life in Victorian England – at the general level the changing fortunes of the Cumbrian yeoman farmer and, more particular to JWR's case, the place of the Society of Friends in the religious constellation at that time and in that place.

1 See Appendix.

2 Seatree, George, 'In memoriam – John W. Robinson', *Fell and Rock Climbing Club Journal*, 1:1 (1907), p.7.

3 Recorded in Hankinson, *The First Tigers*, p.63.

4 Seatree, 'In memoriam – John W. Robinson', *Fell and Rock Climbing Club Journal*, 1:1 (1907), p.9.

5 Haskett-Smith, W.P., 'Doe Crag and John Robinson', *Fell and Rock Climbing Club Journal*, 1:3 (1909), p.234.

Part Two: A Dalesman's Life
Chapter 5: A Statesman's House and Farm

The house in which John Wilson Robinson was born on 5 August 1853 was a substantial, stone-built house in the style characteristic of the Lake District then as now - what is known in the vernacular architecture of the Lakes counties as a 'statesman's house'. The Robinsons were a typical example of the Lakeland yeoman farmer family. In a formal legal sense the term 'yeoman' connoted a person with freehold land worth at least forty shillings a year, but it was also more loosely applied to those who held what were called 'estates of inheritance' – a term deriving from medieval forms of land-holding. The Robinsons were a case of the latter. Hence the term 'statesman' (or 'estatesman'), used normally for the yeomanry in the context of the Lakes counties. The statesman-yeoman was a substantial independent farmer working a considerable acreage by himself, with his family and a small number of hired hands and domestic servants. In the directories and gazetteers of his day JWR's father, Wilson Robinson, was listed among the major landowners of Whinfell, distinct from a separate category of 'farmers'. A statesman would normally have had a good education, and a family history in which he could take pride. In social terms he regarded himself as middle-class, though his status was obviously distinct from that of the urban bourgeoisie. Agricultural production was his profession. His life-style, too, was different from that of the city-dweller. He rarely left home, and so had few occasions to spend money on consumption beyond his daily needs and those of his family.

His farming none the less provided a surplus that enabled him to devote some of his time to other pursuits, recreational (as with JWR's climbing activities) or in local government, to which also JWR turned his hand, as had his father before him. We shall see that it allowed Wilson Robinson to give all his children a boarding-school education. It was into a family of a relative prosperity and a high, if not the highest, status that JWR was born.

The five front windows of the house in which the Robinsons dwelled looked out east over the Vale of Lorton, across the river Cocker in the middle distance to Whinlatter beyond. Angled onto it, and facing north across what had formerly been a courtyard was a somewhat smaller house, though with the same number of front windows. These two dwellings, together with an extension of the smaller house which at times was inhabited, two large barns, several other outbuildings and some 166 acres of land comprised the estate of Whinfell Hall. They were home to the Robinson family, a hired man with his wife and daughter who lived in part of the smaller house, and two, possibly three, girls who gave help indoors and out.

Over the lintel of the larger house there was a 'date stone', built into the masonry. It still carries the legend:

W

I   **S**

1734

This records, in cryptic form, that the house was built, or remodeled, in 1734 and was the home of John Wilson and his wife Sarah. John Wilson (the 'I' being the conventional way of writing a J on date stones) was John Wilson Robinson's great-great-granduncle, and it is useful to construct JWR's genealogy around that ancestor.

Until shortly before the date of 1734 (and taking 1600 as a convenient starting point) the houses had belonged to two apparently unrelated Allason families, the larger to Anthony and the smaller to Thomas Allason. That a pair of distinct Allason families should have inhabited the houses is not as coincidental as it may seem. From at least the early sixteenth century and until into the nineteenth century, people by the name of Allason (or Allison, or Allyson) inhabited the majority of farms in the Whinfell area. Whether our two Allasons were related, then, might have been really a matter of the *degree* of kinship. According to JWR's brother Edmund in his correspondence the distribution of the fields between the two homesteads suggested a partition by a father between two sons, but he held that there was no firm evidence for this.

Thomas Allason's grandson Richard, in the smaller house, died a bachelor in 1720. Faced with the problem of inheritance he had partly bequeathed and partly sold the house in 1714 to his nephew, John Wilson (the son of his sister Jane), on condition that he could live on in it for the rest of his life. Presumably the Wilson family thereupon moved into the house. John Wilson had obviously had some training in the law, as we know that he was a 'conveyancer' and employed himself in drawing up legal documents.

Twenty years later his son, also confusingly named John Wilson, married Sarah Walker of Dean, but by this time the Wilsons had taken the step of buying the larger house next door, and the young couple moved into it after a substantial renovation of the building. With this we arrive at the date stone that he placed over the lintel, shown above: W for Wilson, I (=J) for John, S for Sarah, and 1734 for the date of the house's major remodeling.

This complex story, taking place four generations before JWR's time, is recorded in this date stone together with two others. The second stands over the entrance to the smaller house. Since Richard Allason was a bachelor, the initial of a wife is missing, and the stone reads simply:

RA 1677

The date again records the reconstruction of his house, at a date before that of the remodelling of the main house.

To complete the picture, the third in this collection of date stones stands not over a lintel, but by the side of the entrance to the larger house. It carries the initials of the previous proprietors, the unrelated Allason – Japhet – and his wife Elizabeth. Presumably John Wilson, not wanting to throw the existing date stone away, gave it the honour of a place by the door, if no longer over it. It reads:

A

1   **E**

1698

This time, the A stands for Allason, I for Japhet, and E for his wife Elizabeth (née Richardson of Brow). Just why Wilson should be remodeling a house that had been either built or remodeled only 36 years earlier is unclear, but a possible answer lies in the description below of this period as one of intense building activity.

With the consolidation of the two farms into a single property

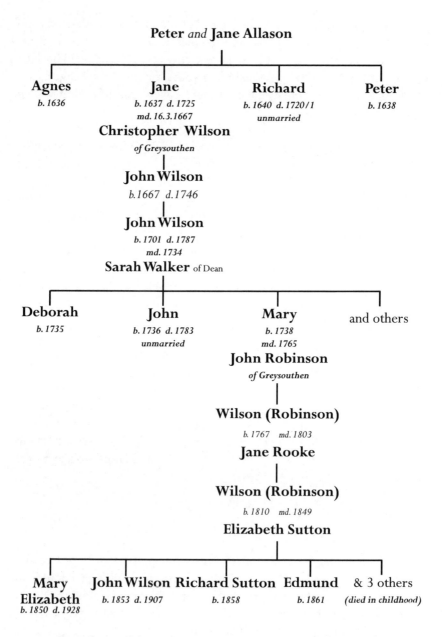

Peter *and* **Jane Allason**

Agnes
b. 1636

Jane
b. 1637 d. 1725
md. 16.3.1667
Christopher Wilson
of Greysouthen

Richard
b. 1640 d. 1720/1
unmarried

Peter
b. 1638

John Wilson
b. 1667 d. 1746

John Wilson
b. 1701 d. 1787
md. 1734
Sarah Walker of Dean

Deborah
b. 1735

John
b. 1736 d. 1783
unmarried

Mary
b. 1738
md. 1765
John Robinson
of Greysouthen

and others

Wilson (Robinson)
b. 1767 md. 1803
Jane Rooke

Wilson (Robinson)
b. 1810 md. 1849
Elizabeth Sutton

Mary Elizabeth
b. 1850 d. 1928

John Wilson
b. 1853 d. 1907

Richard Sutton
b. 1858

Edmund
b. 1861

& 3 others
(died in childhood)

Genealogy of the Wilsons and Robinsons of Whinfell Hall

effected by John Wilson junior, with the rebuilding of both houses, and with various acquisitions made by Richard Allason and both John Wilsons, Whinfell Hall and its land reached the dimensions and acquired the physical appearance that it had when JWR was born in 1853. By then two further generations of the family had lived there, the two John Wilsons, senior and junior, being followed by a pair of Wilson Robinsons, senior and junior. The change of surname from Wilson to Robinson came about through the marriage of the younger John Wilson's niece Mary to a John Robinson of Greysouthen, some six miles to the north-west of Whinfell Hall. For a second time the name of the proprietor of Whinfell Hall had changed through a marriage, from Allason to Wilson and finally to Robinson.

Examining genealogies can be rewarding for those who figure in them, but rather less so for those who do not. That said, JWR's forebears since the seventeenth century were Quakers (the Allasons of both houses had 'joined Friends' at the birth of the movement) and there are particular reasons why genealogy should be important to the Friends. As a group whose dissenting views had distanced it from 'the world', and which had suffered persecution because of those views, it was important for the group to ensure its cohesion. Family linkages became correspondingly important. Should what has been presented here be unclear, a simple family tree is given on page 78.

The restructuring of the two houses took place at a very particular time in the history of Lakeland. From the middle of the seventeenth century the Lake District counties came to be endowed rather abruptly with the architectural landscape familiar today, with its stone-and-slate 'statesman's' houses. The period from around 1650 has come to be known as the 'great rebuilding'. Until that point houses in the Lake District had been predominantly built on what was called the 'cruck' system, in which the frame of the house consisted of two or a row of timber arches formed by large curved beams tied at the apex and mounted on a base. These served as an armature for the walls and the roof.[1]

The 'great rebuilding' in the Lakes counties has been attributed to two main causes. The first was the development of the woollen industry, in which the region was a prominent beneficiary. The second was the evolution of the Scottish factor, which had been a recurring source of social disruption with obvious effects on the local architecture. It was, for example, to protect themselves from marauding bands and armies from the north that the Cumbrians constructed the square 'pele' towers that still stud the north of the county and into Scotland. In the event of an attack a local community – or at least the better-fortuned part of it - could withdraw into the tower and withstand a limited siege. The three storeys of the towers were designed to accommodate the cattle on the ground floor, the victuals for man and beast on the middle floor, with the living quarters for the humans on the top level. These strong and concentrated points of protection were surrounded by far less substantial buildings constructed with an awareness that they might have to be abandoned should the worst befall. By the end of the seventeenth century the tide of invasion had turned, and a population of better-off individuals could build for a more secure future. That said, many of the more substantial subsequent farming homesteads were built in the form of a square, with a central court or farmyard surrounded by buildings on its four sides, with few openings on the outer side, many of them 'slit holes' – an arrangement that clearly combined farming efficiency with considerations of keeping the Scots at bay.

Before concluding on the consolidation of the Whinfell Hall houses in 1734 it is worth recording a particular episode of some tangential interest. John Wilson junior extended the property by purchasing a dwelling on the fell above Whinfell Hall known as the Browe, or the Browe House, bought at auction in 1772. He had previously agreed with a neighbour, Isaac Sibson, to bid jointly, on the understanding that a little under a quarter of the land would be sold on to the latter after the auction, with the house itself being incorporated into the Whinfell Hall holding. The point of historical interest is that the vendor of Browe House was Ann Christian, the mother of Fletcher Christian, the Bounty mutineer. The mutineer himself, however, was born and raised at Moorland Close, some three miles to the northwest of Whinfell Hall.

A second point of some historical interest is that JWR's brother Edmund recalls in his correspondence that part of the Browe building collapsed during his childhood. He recalls also that among the trees near the house was a small leveled patch, oval in shape, and measuring

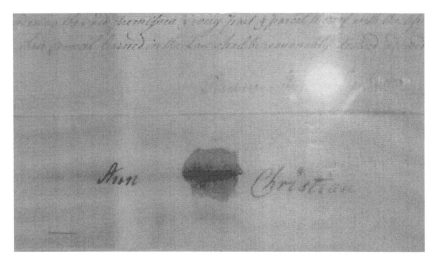

The signature and seal of Ann Christian, the mother of Fletcher Christian the Bounty mutineer. They appear on the conveyance of Browe House to John Wilson junior in 1772.

'perhaps twelve feet by ten'. It was reputed to have been a cock-pit. Cock-fighting, once widespread in the Lakes, had largely died out by JWR's time, leaving occasional recalcitrant cases and – as apparently at the Browe House – archeological remains.

John Wilson's son (yet another John) died unmarried in 1783. As noted, his sister Mary had married a John Robinson and had gone to raise a family with him a little distance away in Greysouthen. Mindful, no doubt, of questions of inheritance, old John Wilson formed a particular attachment to their little son, and indeed young Wilson Robinson went to live with his grandfather at Whinfell Hall in 1772 at the age of five. Grown to maturity, and having married in 1803, Wilson Robinson followed in his grandfather's footsteps by giving his own son the same Christian name as himself.

The century and half from John Wilson's consolidation of the property in 1734 to the death of his great grandson Wilson Robinson the younger in 1899 represents the high period of Whinfell Hall's fortunes. It was, however, a period of change, and by the time JWR entered on his inheritance in the concluding year of the nineteenth century, the life of Lake District farmers had been transformed. By then the enclosure of the commons had already made its impact on the Lakeland landscape, somewhat later than in the greater part of England, and was transforming the whole system of land tenure, with its curious medieval legal basis in 'customary tenure'.

JWR was not, in strict legal terms, the owner of Whinfell Hall when he inherited it in 1899. It will be recalled that he and his forebears held a good part of the property as tenants of the lord of the manor, in this case the holder of the 'honour' of Cockermouth. Customary tenure of the land, its origin lying in earliest medieval times, was in formal terms still prevalent during JWR's lifetime, though the process of enfranchisement, which led to today's vestiges in ground-rent or chief-rent, was already well advanced, and already much of the Whinfell Hall land had been enfranchised.

Customary tenure was in medieval times a form of vassalage, when the majority of tenants in Cumberland were 'tenants at will' or 'customary tenants', holding their land at the will of the lord 'according to the custom of the manor'. The chief obligations of the tenant under this system were the payment of rent and, on specific occasions, of a fine. Fines were incurred both when the lord of the manor or the tenant died, and when the holding was transferred to another tenant. In certain cases, though not in that of the manor of Whinfell, the tenant was required on these same occasions to present to the lord of the manor his or her finest live animal – an obligation known as the heriot (heriots were still being claimed by landlords in the Lakes Counties at mid-point of the nineteenth century). The tenant could be obliged also to contribute labour through 'boon-days', involving ploughing, harrowing and haymaking for example. Thus, in medieval times, in the manor of Whinfell, tenants had owed one day's ploughing, one of harrowing and one of reaping.[2]

The collecting of rents and the payment of fines or heriots was supervised by a manorial court. At a meeting of the 'court baron', surrender of land was recorded and new tenants were 'admitted', offences against manorial rules were punished, issues relating to the administration of the manor were dealt with, complaints were heard and disputes settled. The lord's steward officiated at the meeting. All free tenants were obliged to attend meetings of the court, to act as jurors. Failure to attend without providing a get-out payment - was penalised ('amerced').

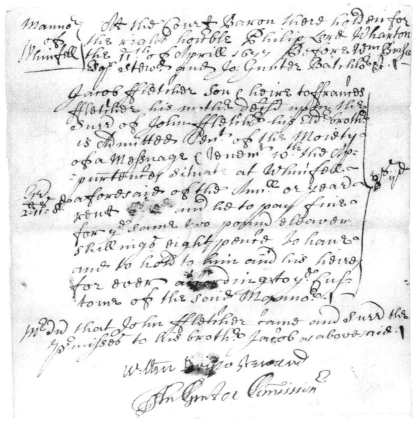

The earliest recorded admittance in the deeds of Whinfell Hall, though it refers, in fact, to the Browe House, which was later incorporated into the holding.

An historical account of this kind gives the impression that the tenant was not too secure in his tenancy and could be evicted at the lord's will at any time, or at the least at those moments when admittances were renewed. That no doubt was the formal position, but 'custom' over time had worked in the tenants' favour, inheritance playing a great part in this evolution. Tenancies had passed from one generation of a family to another, each new tenant assuming the charges and responsibilities of the former and each transition contributing to a sense of permanence

Admittance of John Wilson Robinson in 1901

buttressed by the formality of the court. Already in 1625 a decision of the King's Bench had confirmed tenants in their customary tenure with a right of inheritance. Tenancy of the land was to give way in importance to title-by-purchase of a building situated on that land, and lordship of a manor came to have only a sentimental or antiquarian value. None the less, in strictly formal terms customary tenure was still the norm in JWR's day.

The documents shown on pages 83 and 84 are examples of admittances to customary tenure. The first is the earliest recorded admittance in the deeds of Whinfell Hall, relating in fact to Browe House before its incorporation into Whinfell Hall (the Fletchers mentioned thus being forebears of Fletcher Christian). The second concerns John Wilson Robinson himself and is dated 29 October 1901, by which time the system of customary tenure had largely passed into history, leaving only vestiges of which this document of 1901 is an example. The document is useful in showing the court's custom of marking the fine and the rent in the

84

margins.

Courts, rents and fines summon up an image of forbidding formality, which is belied by contemporary accounts of meetings of manorial courts. Walter Head records one such account from the *West Cumberland Times* of 30 May 1874: 'The tenants met at Kirkstyle and after being relieved of their rents by Mr.Waugh [presumably the steward of the manor] they sat down to a substantial dinner provided by Mrs. Pearson. After dinner, the Court Leet or Lord's Court was held, when the fines due on the death of the late Mr. M Marshall were assessed ... After dinner the tenants drew up till't fire and t'crack and t'jokes went round under the cheering influence of Mrs. Pearson's potential liqueurs'.[3]

Thus, over time, what had originally been a form of vassalage had come to give the tenant a security equivalent to that offered by freehold. It was a structure of land holding that underpinned the status of the independent 'statesmen' of the region, who by the time of both John Wilsons, not to mention the subsequent pair of Wilson Robinsons, had become a rural middle class of yeoman farmers. The composition of the Whinfell Hall land holding illustrates, like the layers of an archeological site, the various phases through which land tenure passed in the Lakes counties. Of the total of a little over 166 acres in the younger Wilson Robinson's day, 30 acres were held as 'ancient freehold', 67 were 'subject to the exceptions, reservations and other matters and things contained in the Act of Parliament for enclosing lands within the Manor of Whinfell', while 69 were held in customary tenure of Baron Leconfield, Lord of the Manor of Whinfell.

With this younger Wilson Robinson, born in 1810, we arrive at JWR's immediate family. Wilson was an only child, born late in his mother's life. In the view of JWR's brother Edmund, to whose family memoirs we owe most of the detail of this section, it was because his mother did not want to part with him that Wilson Robinson was kept at home as a child, although he was later to send all his own children away to school to secure a Quaker education for them. Instead, he attended the village school until 'he knew more than the teacher', complementing what he was learning at school by studying also at home.

Apparently he had wanted to be a solicitor, but since he was an only child his mother was as little inclined to let him seek his fortune in that direction as she had been to let him be sent away to school.[4] For his part, Edmund Robinson recalls his father as 'studious and no farmer or money-maker', communicating little about money matters, even with his wife Elizabeth. It was apparently she, in any case, who was the manager. So it was that Wilson Robinson lived on the farm all his life and farmed it himself after his marriage in 1849, though apparently the farm itself had been rented for a period before that. He undertook extensive work laying down a good length of drainage, improving his land, and maintaining the banks of the river Cocker upstream from Whinfell Hall, in collaboration with his neighbour at Littlethwaite.

He was also active in the community, serving for many years as road supervisor for the parish, in those days before the Parish Councils Act gave charge of the roads to the new district councils. His choice of which projects to favour led to his public-spirited efforts in this sphere to be at times less appreciated than he might have wished. It appears that after he had filled in some depressions in the fell road to Mosser, some of the taxpayers grumbled that he was 'fixing the road to take his wife to meetings', that being indeed the route that the family followed when going to the Friends' Meeting House at Pardshaw.

JWR's great climbing companion George Seatree remembers Wilson Robinson as 'a kindly, quiet-living, unobtrusive country gentleman, a close student of the literary associations of the Lake District, and possessing a keen appreciation of the beauties of nature surrounding his home'.[5] There is also a persistent and rather less generous notion in the collective memory of Edmund's descendants that Wilson Robinson spent most of his time reading.

He was a keen walker, thoroughly familiar with the fells, and fond of recording his outings with paper and pencil. JWR himself told Seatree that as far back as 1824 his father, as noted, had discovered and sketched Napes Needle on the flank of Gable – Robinson *père* here offering a gentle pre-echo of the opening up of the Lakeland climbs that his illustrious son was to share in effecting.

Wilson Robinson's wife, Elizabeth Sutton, had come from a wealthier family in Carlisle, and now had to live within reduced means. The Sutton family, like the Robinsons, were Quakers, their pedigree in this respect reaching back to the Society of Friends' earliest days, several of her ancestors having served as 'Public Friends' or Ministers. Elizabeth herself had had a Quaker schooling at Wigton from 1825 to 1828. It was doubtless the close links between the Friends' meetings at Pardshaw and at Carlisle that had provided Wilson Robinson with his bride.

There is no precise record of the uses to which the Whinfell Hall land was put, but a good deal can be inferred from memoirs and the family's correspondence, in addition to what we know about agriculture in general in the area at that time. Today there is scarcely any arable farming in the Vale of Lorton, but then some two thirds of the Whinfell Hall land was apparently under crops. In fact a shift from arable to pastoral farming took place during JWR's lifetime which, we shall see in a later chapter, was to create economic difficulties for the yeoman farmers of the day, but at mid-point in the nineteenth century arable production still predominated on the Whinfell Hall holding. Potatoes, turnips and cereals were grown, with oats being probably the chief cereal crop, followed by barley (bigg, as it was known locally at the time) and wheat. Much of the barley would have been malted on the premises. The amount of wheat grown would not have been great. JWR's brother Edmund tells of their father's going to Aikbank mill on horseback over the fell road with wheat in a sack across the horse's back, which does not bespeak a voluminous harvest. The end of reaping the cereal crop would be marked by what was styled a 'kirn supper'.

The land on the fell-side was used as grazing for sheep, bringing the usual problems of containment and relations with neighbours. This partic- ularly affected an outlying piece of Whinfell Hall land known as Cold Coats. Edmund recalls that Joe Henderson of Littlethwaite had a 'Coldcoats' adjoining, and there was frequent trouble with sheep getting through the fence. 'Old Joe' had a sober view of the local Herdwick sheep: 'If they can find a la'al hole they can git their heads through, they just wink and thrast'.

A moderate holding of cattle is witnessed by the allocation of space to dairying in both the houses. Set in the south-facing wall of the vegetable garden was a bee-bole for the straw beehives, further evidence of Whinfell Hall's self-sufficiency.

A large millpond on the fell above the houses provided water for a wheel on the side of the larger of Whinfell Hall's two barns. This was a

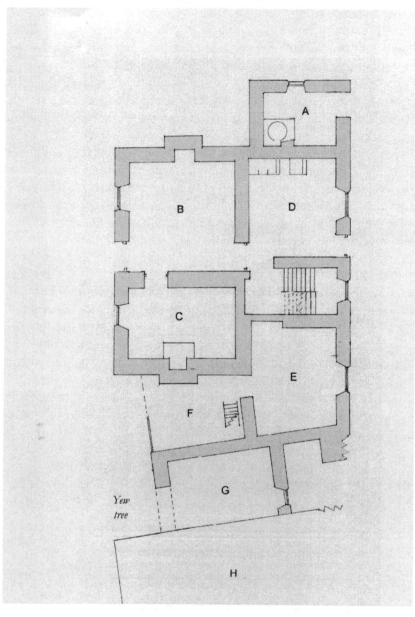

Plan of the farmhouse prior to 1883

'bank barn', the rising ground behind it making possible direct access to an upper floor. We know that the lower level contained a saw bench, the saw having about an 15-inch cut, which was used, among other things, to cut posts for fencing. The timber would have come from the estate. It is recorded that JWR's father was one of the earlier landholders in the area to plant larch. There was a 'Round Plantation' of them in the middle of the fell. Apparently a delegation came from Wales to see the trees because they could not be got to grow in the part of Wales from which the delegation came.

We are fortunate in having a detailed description of the smaller of Whinfell Hall's two houses in the correspondence of JWR's brother Edmund. This was referred to at the time as the 'farm-house'. It accommodated the hired man and his family, but it is the main ground-floor rooms that show the real historical interest.

In an out-house (marked A in the drawing on page 88) was a 'set-pot' - a large vat some 40 inches in diameter, heated over a coal grate and used for cooking feed for the stock. Room B had a floor of large smooth sandstone flags and was used in JWR's day as a laundry. In the other front room (C) flour and other perishables were stored in two large chests, each some three feet wide and five feet long, with movable partitions. Room E was the dairy, lined with sandstone sconces. On these were placed 'leads', or moveable pans – some square and measuring about two feet by three, others round. Room F was used as a cheese-room, with the apple-loft over it, but it had previously housed the mangle. This extraordinary machine, according to Edmund's memoirs, consisted of a very large box, some four feet by eight, filled with cobbles. It was moved to and fro over the base of a heavy frame on hardwood rollers about four inches in diameter, on which were wrapped the sheets or other items to be 'mangled'. The box was hauled over the wooden base by a windlass and ropes. The day of the tumble-dryer had not yet dawned. Finally, the family gig shared room G with a cheese-press, operated in a way somewhat similar to the mangle. In this case pressure was exerted on the cheese by a large boulder in a frame, raised and lowered by an iron screw. Wool and other commodities were stored at a higher level in that room.

It is not clear how much time the master of Whinfell Hall spent physically working on the farm, but his role was chiefly that of manager.

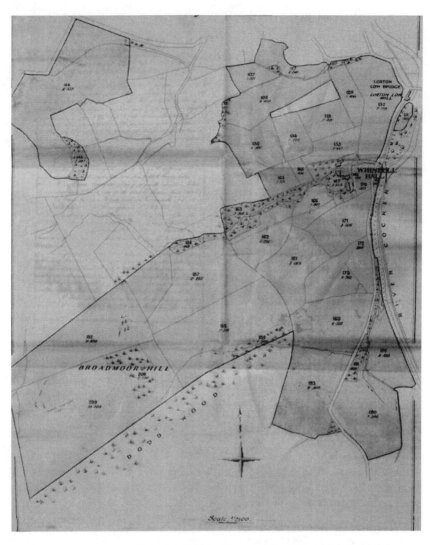

Plan of the Whinfell Hall estate in JWR's day

We have seen that he was able to free himself from these duties to engage in other activities, public and private. We have seen also that a hired man and his family lived in the farmhouse. The hired man's wife helped milk and sometimes worked in the fields and farmyard. Also living in, presumably in the main house, were two girls, one helping in the house and the other an 'out girl'. The latter did some housework, such as washing dishes, cleaning shoes and so on and helped with the washing, while outside she fed the pigs and took a hand with feeding and milking the cattle. In spring and summer she worked in the fields, planting and picking potatoes and taking part in the general mobilisation that hay time and the harvest called for. At harvest time, or possibly for a longer period, a single boy or young man aged 18 or 20 would be hired. Local tradesmen would come to work at Whinfell Hall, but it is not clear how many were employed full-time. That some were is suggested by records that speak of 'the joiners' working the saw-bench.

In a rather different category was the children's governess. It is not known whether she lived in or visited, nor are there any details available of the kind of person that was employed in that capacity. She would, however, undoubtedly have been a Quaker.

Such was the holding from which JWR made his living, and from which he would regularly free himself to join his climbing fellows on the rocks.

1 See Brunskill, R.W., *Vernacular Architecture of the Lake Counties*, London: Faber and Faber, 1974, pp.103-7 for details of the cruck construction system.

2 Winchester, A.J.L., *Landscape and Society in Medieval Cumbria*, Edinburgh, John Donald, 1987, p.65.

3 Head, Walter, 'Manorial records', *Lorton and Derwent Fells Local History Society Newsletter*, No.35, May 2005, p.2.

4 *Extracts from letters written by Edmund Robinson late of Whinfell Hall to J.G.Brooker, 1931-1943*. Typescript in the archives of the Lorton and Derwent Fells Local History Society The material of the remainder of this chapter is drawn almost entirely from this source.

5 Seatree, George, 'In memoriam', *Fell and Rock Climbing Club Journal*, 1:1, 1907, p.4.

Chapter 6:
A Quaker Upbringing

Wilson Robinson was 39 years old when he married Elizabeth Sutton in 1849. The couple's first child, Mary Elizabeth, was born on 16 November 1850. She was to live on into old age, but the second child born, Jane, died at the age of 14, in January 1866. JWR entered the world one year after Jane, on 5 August 1853. We have no record of the circumstances of his birth, since the family records perished in a barn fire in the United States in or near 1906, but he would have been welcomed as the heir presumptive to the Whinfell Hall estate. A further sister, Emily, was born in 1855. She, like Jane, was to die young, at the same age of 14.

On 29 January 1858 a second son was born – Richard Sutton. He and JWR were very close, and Richard was to accompany JWR on many of his climbing excursions. Indeed, Kelly and Doughty credit him with having made the first ascent of the Shamrock Chimneys on Pillar Rock in 1894, which must have been on a visit to Whinfell after his emigration to the United States. Then, on 15 January 1861, a pair of twins was born to the Robinsons – Edmund and Arthur. Arthur, was born 10 minutes after his brother, according to the family bible. He was to die in his fourth year.

All the children were sent away for their schooling. Each of the three schools chosen was run by the Society of Friends. Mary Elizabeth, the eldest of the children, went to the Mount School for girls at York. Her younger brothers Richard and Edmund, and her younger sister Emily until her death in 1869, were sent to Wigton School. This school had been founded in 1815 by the Cumberland General Meeting of the Society of Friends, together with the Scottish Friends, and was situated at first at Highmoor on the outskirts of Wigton. Growing fast in its early years, and accepting non-Friends from the 1820s, it had removed to Brookfield on the other side of town, and the new premises had opened its doors in 1828. The close bonds within the Quaker community are illustrated in the links that are recorded between the teaching staff and the families of the pupils. Wilson Robinson's wife Elizabeth, who had been educated at the school, was later engaged to be married to one of the teachers, Alfred Barter, but

Richard, John Wilson, Edmund and Mary Elizabeth Robinson in 1867

he died before the arranged marriage date, ten years before Elizabeth married Wilson Robinson. JWR attended a different school - Ackworth School in Pontefract, Yorkshire - which had been founded in 1779 by the London Yearly Meeting of the Society of Friends for Quaker boys and girls. He spent two years there, from 1867 to 1869 – that is, from his fourteenth to his sixteenth year.

Until he was 14 JWR was taught by a governess, as indeed were all the children. Whinfell Hall even sported a domestic schoolroom, in a cottage that was an extension of the farmhouse in the direction of the main house, completing the angle between them. This had been a malthouse, but it was converted from that use when Wilson Robinson the younger married and moved his parents in there. After their death it changed its purpose again, and its small parlour became a schoolroom for JWR and his siblings. Edmund tells us that he can remember having been taught by three different governesses. If the governess lived in, she presumably was housed in this cottage. She was aided in her educational duties by 'Mary E.' when she was home from school at York, though she was only three years older than her eldest charge – JWR.

When the children were at home they played with Hannah Simon, the daughter of the hired man, who lived in the farmhouse. They did not, however, play much with the village children. The chief reason for this choosiness was simply that the children of Quaker families did not mix much with those of other families. Edmund adds a second reason. In his terms, he held that he and his siblings were 'middle class', while the village children were mostly 'working class'. The inverted commas are his, and it can be readily understood that these categories would be difficult to apply with any clarity in the area around Whinfell Hall in the middle-to-late nineteenth century. The distance that Edmund felt existed between his family and others is none the less revealing. Not many families in the area could afford, or would expect, to send their children away to a boarding school, but in the case of Quaker families, even at a cost that strained their purse, it would have been justified by the need to give their children an education based on the values of their religious convictions. In any case, the children faced a problem familiar to all those who have been sent away to school. Absence removes them from the local friendship networks and necessarily sets a social distance between them and the children who have stayed at home in the locality.

Fortunately a group of four (for a period more) children constituted a community. For JWR and his sister and brothers, the arrival back at home from school was a moment for collective celebration. They marked it by hoisting a flag at the prominent end of a barn facing, across a large field, anyone crossing the river Cocker and turning up the valley road [1].

As a Quaker family, the Robinsons would go to meeting in the Friends' Meeting House in Pardshaw. Pardshaw lay over the fell behind Whinfell Hall and to its west. Two roads led there. One was steep, and passed over the shoulder of the fell, coming down to Mosser and then on to Pardshaw. It was rough and unsuitable for wheeled traffic, but from its high point it offered a spectacular view over the west Cumbrian coastal plain to the Irish Sea and, to the right, the Solway Firth, with the Scottish hills beyond. The other road skirted the fell, turning left beyond Rogerscale over a humpback bridge at Sandy Beck, and passing through Toddell to Pardshaw. Toddell (its name having evolved over the years from 'Tod Holes' – that is, fox-holes) was the home of another major Quaker family of Whinfell, the Dixons.

The family would usually go to meeting by the higher 'fell road', returning either the same way or by the lower road that led from Brandling Ghyll to the hump-backed bridge at Sandy Beck -- Mirk Lonning (spelled in the record in any number of permutations of Murk, Merk and Mirk with Lonning, Lonnin and Loanen). Writing in 1934 about his early years, the octogenarian Edmund recalled that in his childhood 'one of the interesting features as we returned from meeting at Pardshaw [by the fell road] was to see "Jonah Dixon's Little Man fighting with the wind"'. This was a revolving weathervane on the barn at Toddell, made of wood and representing a soldier of the Peninsular War. Edmund adds that he intended to turn one on his lathe. He recalls also that the shepherd's house on the Mosser side of the summit was known familiarly as 'dry thropple hall', probably 'because of the scarcity of liquor while it was being built'.

At a certain point the family apparently acquired a four-wheeled conveyance, after which they almost always went and returned by Mirk Lonnin. The children also had a small dark brown donkey, named Briton, which they would take it in turns to ride, the others bumping along in the conveyance. The bumping had its special moments. Going over Sandy Beck bridge was always a grand moment for the children. Even better was another humpback bridge at Toddell, with an even sharper hump, because their father would start the horses trotting as the conveyance came down the hill approaching it. Needless to say, the road has today long been improved, and the entertaining hump levelled out. The opportunities for children to experience the keen joy of bouncing over hump-backed bridges are a good deal rarer now than in the days of JWR and his brothers and sisters. At other times Briton the donkey would be harnessed to a green cart, mostly for the children to have fun with around the

Whinfell Hall about 1888

farmstead. The fun was not entirely unalloyed, and Edmund records two occasions on which the donkey gave him a savage kick, one of them resulting in a permanent scar on his temple.

Almost every summer the children used to spend part of their holidays on the coast at Allonby, at the time a small fishing village which functioned in a quiet way as a seaside resort. There they stayed with Sarah Satterthwaite, a relative of the family, in a house attached to the Ship Inn. Edmund tells us that they enjoyed the fresh shrimps at Allonby, but that the herring had to come from elsewhere, because the dumps of slag on the shore at Maryport left by the iron-smelting there had persuaded the herring to feed elsewhere. During one summer holiday the family ventured further afield, when Janet took the three boys to Douglas on the Isle of Man. Mary Elizabeth stayed at home on this occasion to keep house for their father.

It should be clear by this point that the Quaker dimension was a determining factor in many aspects of the life of JWR.

The implantation of the Society of Friends in the Lakes counties

A drawing by JWR of the larger of the Whinfell Hall houses

dates from 1652 when George Fox visited them on his tour of the north west of England. The area has since been regarded as the birthplace of Quakerism. In the fifty years that followed that date the movement grew so strongly that there were 'meetings' no more than eight miles apart on average throughout the entire district.[2] Meetings were, and are, grouped into monthly meetings, and Pardshaw, the meeting that our family attended, was the locus for one of the four monthly meetings in Cumberland at the time.

Pardshaw lies, as noted, at a distance of some four miles to the north-west of Whinfell Hall, over the fell behind the homestead. A prominent feature of the landscape at Pardshaw is the Crag, which rises to over 100 feet above the surrounding ground. Its elevation is enough for it to have served as a pulpit, and the fact that George Fox so used it has given it a certain talismanic status for the Friends – though holding meetings out of doors, in good or bad weather, was a characteristic of the early Quakers, emphasising their rejection of church buildings — termed by them 'steeple houses' — as a distraction from seeking the truth.

George Fox records in his diary a further visit to the area in 1653, when he spoke under the yew tree hailed by Wordsworth as the 'yew tree, pride of Lorton Vale' in a celebrated poem published in 1815. This yew was situated over the river from Whinfell Hall, in the village of Lorton itself where, in a form much reduced by intervening years, it may be visited today.[3] A great many people gathered on that occasion, putting themselves and the famous yew at risk by crowding onto its branches until the tree was full of folk. In consideration of the risk, Fox was persuaded to move the meeting to the village church. The record of the event does not tell us whether or not this recourse to a symbol of the established church caused Fox any particular embarrassment. The choice in any case was made not by him, but by the guardians of public order.

JWR's brother Edmund offers us a condensed description of how the Friends in his time were structured as a religious community. It is brief and schematic but, since it comes from the pen of a member of JWR's family, it has an air of immediacy and is worth presenting here as a statement by a contemporary of how things were at that time. He is addressing the correspondent who was asking him questions about the Quaker families of the area. The abbreviations and the use of capital letters in the original have been retained, but the punctuation has been tidied up.

You ask about Meeting organization, Excuse me if I repeat what you already know. Certain districts, usually a County, sometimes two counties, comprised a Quarterly Meeting. This was subdivided into smaller districts or Monthly Meetings, as Carlisle, Holm, Pardshaw and Caldbeck (It seems to me Strickland was in Westmorland Q.M.) The various individual meetings in each M. Mg. held once a month a business session termed a Preparative Meeting. This meeting managed the financial affairs of the mtg, and such routine Business as had to be sent up to the M. Mtg (held Monthly as the name implies) such as moneys for the work of the latter, couples intending to Marry had to present their intentions before the mtg (in the early days. That practice was discontinued many years ago) [In] cases of insubordination or misconduct Parties had right of appeal to the

Mo.Mtg. I am not sure if Prep. Mtgs handled admission to membership and disownments, but rather think such matters were passed up to the M.Mtg. Representatives (Delegates) were appointed to the M. Mtg. Similarly the M.Mtg dealt but finally [thus in the original - MW], with disownments, marriages, etc. (The marriages were performed in the individual meetings). Appointed Representatives to the Q. Mtg passed up dues etc, and any cases on appeal, etc. The Q. M. in turn passed up matters to the Y. M. any that had to go up [thus in the original – MW] and appointed Representatives. No one received any personal pay or expenses, I think the Queries were read in all the various meetings. Some had to be answered and reported to the superior Mtg, others became known as Unanswered Queries and were very valuable as the means of searching of hearts as to faithfulness, etc. Each individual mtg. also had Elders and Overseers and held mtgs of Ministry and Oversight, reporting to their superior Mtgs. These were exclusive, being only attended by Ministers, Elders and Overseers, The Elders were supposed to be spiritually minded persons, who counseled with the Ministers and others in such matters. The Overseers attended to disciplinary matters, the relief of the poor, etc. etc.

In another place Edmund added that in addition to Quarterly, Monthly and Preparative Meetings there was a Meeting for Sufferings.

The latter was not functioning in my time; at least not in the Quarterly and subordinate Meetings, I am not sure if it was not maintained in London, but probably its work had changed. Whether latterly Peace, Freedmen, etc, came under it I don't know, Originally I suppose they kept some record of the 'sufferings of Friends' by way of imprisonments, destraint for tythes etc. etc. Whether they helped the poorer Friends who suffered destraint or how far their sympathies extended I know not.

The Robinson family used to go to the Quarterly Meeting in Carlisle, staying overnight at Friends' houses. For ordinary 'preparative' meetings, however, as no doubt the two Wilson families before them, they would attend the Pardshaw Meeting House. This had been built in 1729, replacing an earlier structure of 1672. Before the latter date, in fact from 1653, the Friends met in the house of one or other of them. An early record states:

Then [in 1653] frds settled a meeting at the sd Peter Heqd's house, wch was the first meeting yt was settled in Cumberland; & many were convinced of the truth, that the houses Could not Contain them, But they met without Doors, for many years, on a place called Pardshow Cragg, & abundance of People crooded to the meets Peter Head of Pardshaw.

Before long the Pardshaw meeting became so numerous that it began to create other meetings from within itself, held still at Friends' houses. One of these was Whinfell Hall itself. The others were at Pardshaw, Lamplugh and Eaglesfield.[4] In 1748 the overall Pardshaw meeting was still considered the largest country meeting in England.

Richard Hall, whose family lived within four miles of Whinfell Hall and was held in great affection by the Robinsons, recalls the meetings that were held there at the time of JWR's adulthood, though Hall himself was then but a boy. The house, he records, would be full of staid, quietly dressed Quakers, some few even then wearing the ancient dress. The standing of Whinfell Hall in the Quaker community can be assessed by Edmund Robinson's claim that about a third of the Cumberland Quarterly Meeting in JWR's day were descended from the first John Wilson, though it is impossible to verify this claim.

The Meeting House that JWR attended illustrated many of the common features of Quaker meeting houses – a separate small house for women's meetings, a schoolroom, and the burial ground. It was George Fox himself who in 1671, having established men's meetings in each area, encouraged the setting up of women's meetings, though not with separate agendas. This, according to David Butler in his *Quaker Meeting-Houses in the Lake Counties*, was resisted in some places, probably where a view was held that women were not being offered sufficient responsibility.

The meeting house was simplicity itself, with no furniture other than some rows of benches, and a raised platform at the end called the 'minister's stand'. The original Meeting House of 1672 was built actually on the Crag, but by JWR's day all that remained of it was a few stones, the new one having been built nearby. What was originally a school building for the children of Friends had, by JWR's day, become the women's cloakroom.

The close community that the Society of Friends constituted had also an important economic dimension. True, it is difficult to tell whether the Friends preferred to deal with each other rather than with 'the world' simply through the Quaker connection, since the Friends were so numerous in the area, and overlapped strongly with the more general network of economic relations. But it is revealing that JWR's father took wheat to be milled at Aikbank mill on the road to Pardshaw, run by a Friend, rather than taking it to the much nearer Lorton Low Mill.

The Friends' Meetings could acquire property, often through legacies. It was in this way that the Pardshaw Quarterly Meeting acquired a small farm at Eaglesfield, which was left by a Friend to help needy Friends, and another in Millbeck, of which JWR's father was a trustee. Pardshaw Women Friends had a small bequest left them in early days to supply traveling ministers with 'spirits'. In those days such ministers usually came on horseback and sometimes for long distances and might be cold and tired. In later years, when Friends had come to abjure intoxicating liquors entirely, the women used the proceeds to buy doormats and similar things about the meeting house.

The world in which the young John Wilson Robinson grew up was thus a Quaker one. He and his siblings boarded at Quaker schools and they spent part of their summer holidays with Quaker friends and relatives at Allonby. The friendships and even the business contacts of the family were formed to a large extent within a Quaker community conscious of its own identity. We have seen that the Quaker dimension showed through also in JWR's behaviour and attitudes within the rock-climbing fraternity.

In professional terms, however, JWR was a farmer, and as such he was subject to the economic forces that were pressing on the class of yeoman farmers in the second half of the nineteenth century. The next chapter will examine his fortunes in responding to these pressures, and will approach the difficult question of whether his activities on the rocks worked against him in that regard.

1 *Extracts from Letters Written by Edmund Robinson late of Whinfell Hall to J.G.Brooker, 1931-4*. Except where indicated otherwise all references in this chapter are to this source.

2 Butler, David M., *Quaker Meeting-Houses in the Lake Counties*, London and Philadelphia PE: Friends Historical Society, 1978.

3 Baron, Michael G. and Derek Denman, *Wordsworth and the Famous Yew Tree*, Lorton and Derwent Fells Local History Society, 2004.

4 Butler, Quaker Meeting Houses..., p.40, citing the First Publishers of Truth.

Chapter 7:
Married Life and Local Responsibilities

JWR left school at Ackworth in 1869, and embarked on his life as a propertied farmer, helping his father. This was five years before his first meeting with George Seatree in 1874, and 13 years before Haskett-Smith's second visit to Wasdale Head, which was to lead to his memorable partnership with JWR. We have seen that his life as a yeoman farmer afforded JWR the time to make a considerable name for himself as a mountaineer, and in this chapter it will be seen that it enabled him also to play a significant part in local affairs.

These activities beyond the call of farming itself were normal attributes of a yeoman farmer at the time of JWR's birth, and he was able to engage in them to the end of his prematurely curtailed life. However, the times had been changing for the Lakeland yeoman farmer. As in so many other ways, JWR in this respect too lived at an important turning point – and suffered its effects. Whatever part in the eventual loss of Whinfell Hall is attributable to mismanagement of his own affairs, others of his class had been facing a decline in their fortunes. The reasons reached back at least a century, the decline of the yeoman farmer being often put down at its start to the effects of enclosures. Their livelihood had also been affected by the development of factories, which drove out home production. While there is no evidence that the denizens of Whinfell Hall engaged to any great extent in spinning or weaving for the market, they did perform local services such as malting, which also succumbed to industrial development. International factors, too, had played a part, a fall in prices following after the beneficial effects of the Napoleonic wars. The kind of life that JWR led as a Lakeland gentleman farmer was becoming less and less tenable. These general background features of the predicament of Lakeland farmers are taken further below.

It would have been difficult to foresee the ultimately unfortunate effects of these developments in 1869, the date when JWR left school. At that time Wilson Robinson was well in control of the estate. He and his wife were still surrounded by their surviving children, with JWR, the

102

eldest child, beginning to take on some of the work in managing the farm. This domestic state of affairs continued as the years passed, with JWR taking on increasing responsibilities on the estate, and Richard and Edmund growing to adulthood and having to contemplate their futures. However, the rhythm of family life was abruptly broken in 1883 in a sequence of inter-related events. The first was JWR's marriage in that year. This triggered a reconstruction of the farmhouse to accommodate himself and his bride. It also either led directly to, or at least accelerated, the decision of his two younger brothers to emigrate to the United States.

Though all these events fell in a single year, they must have been in gestation for some time. The emigration of Richard and Edmund in particular must have been the culmination of doubts growing over the years. While the family did not subscribe to any principle of primogeniture, John in the nature of things acquired a disproportionate stake in the family holding. As his bother Edmund put it much later in a letter to a friend, John Walker of Saffron Walden, dated 1 December 1910, 'Of course he was older and had worked for Father some years, but he got enough in stock, rents, remittances, implements, etc. to counter-balance that'. In the event their elder brother was to inherit the whole estate, the brothers and their sister receiving no more than moderate legacies from their father. On the other hand it was expected that the estate would care for Mary Elizabeth until such time as she married. It was JWR's own marriage, however, that triggered the break-up of the family.

A Cumbrian courtship was said to be a matter of 'seven years and a la'al bit' and the la'al bit could itself be as long as a further seven years. JWR met his future wife Janet for the first time when he was at school at Ackworth. Since he left school in 1869 and his marriage took place in 1883 the la'al bit must have been at least seven years. Eliza Janet Willis had been born to Dr. John and Elizabeth Ann Willis in 1850 in Ackworth, where John Willis was a teacher of languages, mathematics and history at the school. He was born in Wallingford in Berkshire, but grew up in Bradford, while Janet's mother hailed from Woodbridge in Suffolk. They had a further daughter, Florence, who was Janet's junior by seven years. Almost three years older than John, Janet was also a pupil at Ackworth, which accepted both boys and girls. She spent an even shorter time than John as a pupil there – from 1 February 1862 to 26 March 1863 – but the

Tolinfell Hall
Cockermouth
5. IX. 94.

My dear Girls

After the chorus of kind utter-
ances from all of you anent my writing
in this book I feel that the least I can
do is to comply with your wishes — I
shall really be delighted to have the privi-
lege of seeing these interesting letters, &
as it seems impossible for me to keep
up a correspondence with all I
shall welcome gratefully this method
of keeping in touch. If at any time
you tire of your new member you have
only to drop her, & she will bear you
no grudge. I hope the photo. idea will
be developed & further carried out — It
is most interesting to see Emily's & Lucy's
bairns. How clever & executive you

Two pages from Janet Robinson's collective diary, The Budget.

mothers must get in keeping pace with the manifold requirements of our mercurial offspring. I can sympathise with Bella Webb's absorption in house & husband — & in her interest in gardening — I, who only have the help of a weeding-boy (except for a few days in spring) find plenty of hard, but very interesting & healthful, work in the garden. But while our hay & corn crops are being gathered, the poor garden gets scant attention — & the weeds laugh me to scorn every time I run out to get rhubarb or mint, or to cut a few flowers for a friend. Last Monday we gave our "Kirn Supper" — w? is to celebrate the end of the reaping — (For its origin see "Forty Years in a Moorland Parish") So now there is a lull, for there is no more field work for my maid — & consequently less serving of tables for her mistress.

Willis family lived at the school, and it was when she was no longer a pupil that John was admitted, so that the attachment must have developed through contacts at the Willis abode. Shortly after John left the school the Willis family moved back to Bradford. There Janet, then aged 20, worked as a governess though still living at home. In 1878 she left Bradford to become a schoolmistress at Sidcot School in Winscombe in Somerset. Since her marriage to JWR took place in 1883, the courtship must have been conducted at a distance. Like Ackworth, Sidcot is a school run by the Friends. As noted, the links within the Quaker community in England – as indeed in the whole Anglo-Saxon world – were strong and correspondingly took less account of distance than was the norm in the general population.

JWR's marriage to Janet was celebrated on 20 June 1883, but no details of the occasion have survived. It must have been a turbulent moment in the lives of the Robinson family, experienced differently by its various members. The joy and satisfaction of JWR and his bride must have been qualified in the case of his mother and father by growing concern over the marital prospects of Mary Elizabeth, then aged 32. For Richard and Edmund the marriage must have served as yet another sharp reminder of their precarious position as younger brothers.

JWR's wife Janet reveals something of herself in a circular diary that she kept with some of her former pupils whom she had been teaching at Sidcot School before her marriage. It was called *The Budget*. Even if we make allowances for her feeling it necessary to maintain her tutorial style in her contributions to the diary, she was clearly a person of literary inclinations, as far as her housekeeping duties and the making of the butter permitted. She quotes Browning extensively, and she urges her former charges to read Emerson, to whom she has 'suddenly awoken'. We see in her entries to the diary someone for whom living with a 'mission' can bring problems and yet who belongs to a world where people with missions are valued. 'Are breadth and impartiality always incompatible with intensity and strong convictions?' she asks, answering: 'I hope not – but if so give me *breadth*! "Build thee more stately mansions, O my soul!" etc.etc.'

In view of JWR's ambivalent attitude to the competitive side of rock-climbing, noted above, it is interesting to find in one of Janet's entries in

Eliza Janet Willis, whom JWR married in 1883

the diary, three years after JWR's walk to rival the peak-bagging exploit of the Tucker family, a very forthright view on competition in sport. It occurs in the context of her discovery of the pleasures of cycling. This was the moment when the practice of riding on two wheels was in its infancy. Apparently she was ahead of her correspondents: 'I did not expect it would be left to the oldest writer in these chronicles to be the first to sing the praises of the wheel!...Whether it is a certain cure for rheumatism, varicose veins etc. etc., as alleged, remains to be proved, but sure I am that it is a wonderful cobweb sweeper – and in it is to be found part of the secret of perpetual youth.' But she adds, 'I totally disapprove of and abhor all *racing*, and breaking of records, especially for women. I shall have attained the height of my ambition if I ever win in a 'tortoise race' where the prize goes to the last to come in to goal'.

Did Janet take any part in JWR's activities on the fells? Apparently she did, though not very often. The visitor's book of the Tyson's hotel in Wasdale records that JWR and Mrs Robinson stayed there on 24 and 25 June 1884, and for three days in August 1887 they stayed in the hotel with Mary Elizabeth and a party of Tynesiders. On the latter occasion they were taken up Pillar Rock, and we are told that 'a rope was not used and the ladies came down without assistance'. JWR's diary records that Janet went up Pillar with him again in August 1901.

As for what Whinfell Hall was like at the time when JWR was managing it, we have a somewhat indirect contemporary account in one of the novels of Oliver Macdonell. Macdonell lived at Whinfell Hall with JWR and Janet for a few years as a paying boarder when a boy. He was 12 years old when he first arrived in 1891. JWR's brother Edmund made a visit to the house from the United States in that year, and commented in his correspondence that he found Oliver a very nervous child. 'We felt sorry for him many times, the way Janet raked him' – though we shall see that this does not entirely represent Janet's relationship with her lodger (to rake someone in Cumbrian parlance is to give them a hard time). Though Oliver was only 12 years old at the time, he was apparently taken up Pillar Rock by JWR in the very first year of his arrival in Whinfell Hall. In his *Thorston Hall: a tale of Cumberland farms in the old days*, published in 1936, Macdonell uses Whinfell Hall as his model. It is a work of

THORSTON HALL

*A Tale of Cumberland Farms
in the Old Days*

by

O. S. Macdonell

Author of *George Ashbury* (7th Imp.)

SELWYN & BLOUNT, PATERNOSTER HOUSE,
PATERNOSTER ROW – – – LONDON, E.C.4

The title page of Oliver Macdonell's novel 'Thorston Hall'.

fiction (its plot recounting the suffering of a Quaker girl whose father forbids her to marry 'into the world'), but the house and grounds as described are very much like they are today and must have been then, and the author adds some social details which are historically accurate:

> Some way from the [Lorton Low] Mill, and at a little distance from the road, was a farm. The house was plain and square, with whitewashed walls and small mullioned windows ... Robert Thorston was a yeoman farmer, or 'Statesman' as such were called in his part of the world; he owned the land and farm on which he worked. ...There was no need to travel, or to be interested in places far away. Robert and his neighbours were simple folk, and the only mode of life they knew was a very simple one; all the necessities for it could be got locally. Practically all the food eaten on the farm was grown upon it. The clothes that men and women wore were mostly woollen; the wool of the dale was spun, woven and made up into garments in the neighbourhood. ...
> The house was not large, and made no pretence of being ornamental or picturesque, but it had a plain substantial look. It faced northeast, and so turned its back to the south-west storms, and also to the view of the mountains and the sunshine. In front of the house was a garden, where were a few neglected flowerbeds, paths covered with coarse gravel and stones, and plots of somewhat rough grass. On the south side of the garden was a very large and old yew tree; behind this was a row of buildings consisting of two cottages [in reality the farmhouse and adjacent cottage - MW] and farm outbuildings. To the north of the house and garden was the little beck, where water rushed, or gently rippled over stones, according to whether rain had fallen or not. Across the beck were several small bridges, made of flat slabs of stone; and beyond these were a long low barn and a walled-in kitchen garden. Behind the house was a wood, where large trees grew on either side of the beck; the wood extended up the fell that was to the west.[1]

The house described is clearly the main house, though the young Oliver would presumably have lived in the converted farmhouse, where JWR and Janet lived. Edmund Robinson claims in his memoirs that the old yew tree was mentioned in a deed of about 1600 as the 'great yew tree'. In his day, and therefore JWR's, the old trunk was about four feet in diameter at its base, though it was much decayed at the level of the higher branches.

We learn from Janet's circular diary that for her Oliver Macdonell was in fact more than a lodger. Having no children of her own, she clearly invested a good deal of affection in the future writer. 'Some of you know my boy, Oliver', she wrote in *The Budget*. 'He was with us many years, and felt quite like a son to me'. It is clear, also, that the circular diary was performing something of a similar role, and there is the same poignancy in the good wishes she sends to her former charges on the birth of their children, whom Janet sees as 'my grandchildren'.

At some point during the period when his marriage to Janet Willis was being projected, JWR gained his father's consent to reconstruct the farmhouse with a view to establishing it as the family home for Janet and himself. It will recalled that his great-uncle Richard Allason had earlier remodelled the house, placing his date stone of 1677 over the lintel of the main entrance. This further renovation was apparently less extensive, but it involved none the less raising the roof by some two feet, and extending the eastern gable end towards the road by about four feet. This made room for a passage to be created leading from the main entrance between the two downstairs rooms, in conformity with the Lake District vernacular architecture for small houses.

This reorganisation of the Whinfell Hall holding meant that the hired man and his family had to be moved out of the farmhouse. They were rehoused in the cottage which had earlier served as a school-room for JWR and his sister and brothers. The renovation presumably also meant that the uses to which the farmhouse had been put, as described by Edmund, were thereafter either catered for elsewhere or not catered for at all, though there is no record to tell us which. This is unfortunate, since it is clear that during JWR's stewardship the economic viability of Whinfell Hall came into question, and it would be useful to know how much of that to attribute to general region-wide causes, and how much to the individual decisions and choices of JWR himself. Taking out of use a major slice of the space used for production could have meant either that production had diminished, or that the Robinsons had opted to run down their farming interests. In either case JWR's rock-climbing activities cannot have been a factor in the decision, since in 1883 he had only just made the acquaintance of the Wasdale Head visitors, and the planning of the farmhouse renovation must have got under way even before that date.

JWR's brothers, Edmund and Richard Robinson.

The reconstruction of the farmhouse and JWR's marriage brought to a head the issue of his brothers' futures. On leaving school the elder brother, Richard, had been apprenticed to the architect's firm of Myers,Veevers and Myers in Preston, following its civil engineering course.[2] Thereafter, he worked at Cockermouth Castle for a few years doing engineering work. Edmund himself would have liked to be a solicitor, but his father, having paid the premium for elder brother Richard's apprenticeship, and having had to support Richard in Preston during it, was ill-inclined to support a similar training for the younger brother. Instead he seems to have stayed at home for the most part, helping run the farm. We know that for at least one whole year he went to work in Aspatria with a relation, John Brockbank, whose agricultural methods Edmund found worth studying.

When Richard was 25 and Edmund 22 they left Whinfell Hall to seek their fortune abroad. It was no doubt the Quaker dimension that turned their minds towards the United States as a destination for starting a new life. The establishment in 1682 of William Penn's colony of Pennsylvania as a refuge for persecuted Friends had effectively created a Quaker diaspora, in which Friends were as much at home on one side of the Atlantic as on the other. For the younger sons of Friends emigration to America was the equivalent in that day of the military commission or a curate's living for the younger sons of the Establishment aristocracy. Indeed, four of the children of a forebear of Edmund and Richard, Christopher Wilson, had emigrated to the United States some hundred years earlier.

On arriving in the United States the brothers almost immediately separated in Des Moines, Iowa. Richard then moved around the country doing engineering and mining work, living for 30 years in Tacoma near Seattle, before moving on to Canada. Edmund records that his brother worked for many concerns that went broke and failed to pay him. Eventually Edmund took Richard under his wing in California.

Edmund himself, meanwhile, took the Civil Service examination and went into the US public land service, spending a little less than 30 years in that employment. On 19 January 1988 he married Maranda Hadley, and daughters and a son were in due course born to them.

With the departure of the brothers, the family at Whinfell Hall comprised Wilson Robinson, by then 73 years of age, his wife Elizabeth and Mary Elizabeth in the main house, with John and Janet in the refurbished former farmhouse. The younger couple had no children to enliven the scene. For the next 16 years it was JWR himself who had effective charge of running the farm, with the help, as before, of the hired hand, the domestic servants and occasional further hired labour.

His activities on the rocks, and the prominence they have acquired in our received knowledge of JWR, inevitably steer our attention away from what must have been the chief call on his time – the management of a substantial agricultural business. It is clear, none the less, that JWR was able to free himself from purely farming concerns to quite an extent. To his rock-climbing must be added also the work he took on in local affairs, as befitted one of the major landholders of the Cockermouth area. His readiness to assume responsibilities in that field, and indeed his political stances as well, were clearly influenced by his Quaker upbringing and convictions. Being a great advocate of peace and temperance he gave active support to the Lorton Christian Temperance Society and the Band of Hope. He personally remained a teetotaller all his life. Another of his concerns close to home was the Lorton Reading Room.

Beyond the village level he took an active part in local government, sitting on the Rural District Council and representing his parish for many years on the Cockermouth Union of Board of Guardians, which historically had charge of the poor under legislation dating back to 1601. The Cockermouth Poor Law Union had come into being formally on 1 December 1838, with an elected Board of Guardians, drawn from its constituent parishes. JWR, like his father before him, would have been the Brigham representative. In 1840-3, during his father's turn of duty, the Union had built a new workhouse on a site between Gallowbarrow and Sullart Street in Cockermouth. The first part of it was opened in June 1841, but a fever hospital and an additional eastern wing were added in 1847. In 1846-7 it had about 230 inmates.[3]

This, of course, was before the Boards of Guardians were finally abolished in the Local Government Act of 1929, but JWR's involvement in local affairs fell squarely in the period when reform of the administration of country areas was a major preoccupation of the English political class.

He was 31 years old when the County Franchise Act of 1884 extended to the counties the household suffrage, which already existed in the boroughs, thereby almost doubling the number of Parliamentary voters in England and Wales. Further reform came four years later with the Local Government Act of 1888 which took the radical step of creating county councils and transferring to them the administrative powers that the Justices of the Peace had historically held. Finally the Parish Councils Bill that resulted in the further Local Government Act of 1894 introduced local self-government into rural parishes and brought order into the chaos of existing boards and *ad hoc* bodies by gathering into the hands of district councils a number of administrative functions such as the maintenance of roads, and abolishing others. Through his work on the local rural district council, JWR's life was thus lived at a fulcral point, in this as in so many other fields. As a Gladstonian Liberal he supported the reform programme at national level. He was a keen admirer, and also a personal friend, of Sir Wilfrid Lawson, MP, the avuncular chairman of the Maryport and Carlisle Railway, a leading Cumberland radical teetotaller and son of the owner of Littlethwaite, the property neighbouring the Robinsons' upstream on the river Cocker. It will be recalled also that

JWR's close friend, George Seatree, shared these Liberal views, and had seen the inside of a prison for his energy in demonstrating them.

These activities in local administration naturally extended to the farming sphere. We know, for example, that he served for a time as estimator of crops for a district in Cumberland. Nor did the Quaker community itself escape from JWR's sense of social responsibility. He acted as clerk of the Monthly and Preparative meetings of the Pardshaw Friends and, as with so many of his activities, he extended his action beyond the locality. Thus we find him acting as Agent for Ackworth School. This meant spreading information about the advantages of an education at Ackworth among Friends while keeping up-to-date prospectuses available for parents of children not connected with the Society, making sure that information was known to Friends about bursaries available, and other such promotional responsibilities. He also sat for a short time on the Committee of Wigton School, which his two brothers had attended.[iv]

In short, JWR lived the life of a gentleman farmer appropriate to the circumstances of his time. While he and his wife worked personally on the farm, they were aided in their tasks by hired help and domestic servants. JWR had time available not only for his climbing activities, but also for an involvement in local affairs that no doubt was expected of a person of his standing. But the circumstances were changing and presenting him with challenges that were to test his business skills as a farmer, and his personal ability to cope with those challenges.

1 Macdonell, Oliver, *Thorston Hall: a tale of Cumberland farms in the old days*, London: Selwyn and Blount, 1936, pp.17, 24/5.

2 *Extracts from Letters Written by Edmund Robinson late of Whinfell Hall to J.G.Brooker1931-1943*, typescript, held in the archive of the Lorton and Derwent Fells Local History Society. Unless stated otherwise, all references in this chapter are to this source.

3 Bradbury, J.B., *A History of Cockermouth*, Chichester: Phillimore, 1981, p.96.

4 Information provided by Ackworth School.

Chapter 8:
Tribulations

The rhythm of JWR's life followed remarkably closely the development of rock-climbing in the English Lake District. He was walking the fells and making the acquaintance of early rock-climbers before he first climbed Pillar Rock in 1882, the year of Haskett-Smith's second visit to Wasdale Head. In that year he was 29 years old. At that point his father would still have been very active and carrying the responsibility for running the Whinfell Hall farmstead. The following 17 years constituted the main period of JWR's involvement in the birth of rock-climbing in the Lake District. This was also the heroic early phase of Lakeland climbing, before it evolved into a consolidated movement, marked by the creation of the Fell and Rock Climbing Club in 1907. Looked at from a climbing perspective, JWR's career on the rocks was keeping pace with the development of the sport, and was to culminate in his nomination as Vice-President of the new-born club.

However, when the period is examined from the point of view of his life as a dalesman and farmer, a rather different picture emerges, this time not one of participation in a new-born thing with a promising future ahead of it. On the contrary, these were years of decline in Lakeland agriculture, and particularly of the yeoman class, and it is to be imagined that he was keenly aware of this contrast. Personal factors, too, played their part. The emigration of his brothers, the fact that he and his wife Janet had no offspring to build a future for the farm on, and finally the death of his parents, both in the final year of the century, must have weighed heavily on him. It is clear, in fact, that the negative factors in his personal life were eclipsing, for him, his success in the climbing sphere, though that is not how it appeared to his climbing partners. They did not notice that the year of 1899 brought a marked reduction in his climbing activities, but by then a turning point had already been reached in his personal life.

It was in 1895 that JWR took the step that would lead before long to his severing his link with the homestead of his forebears. He rented an office in Keswick and set up as a land agent and auctioneer, while continuing for a further five years to live at Whinfell Hall with his parents and his sister and to manage the farm. Among the landowners for whom he acted as agent were R.D.Marshall of Castlerigg Manor near Keswick and John Musgrave of Wasdale Hall. It may be imagined that the personal element in at least the second of these relationships was quite strong. Musgrave's land held, after all, some of the prime climbs on which JWR had made his climbing reputation, including the Napes flank of Gable. A certain Mr Tact and a Miss Gates also feature in the record of those to whom JWR gave financial advice in this episode of his life.[1]

It is here that the lack of information about his personal life begins to be really serious. Already in 1883, the year of his marriage and the emigration of his brothers, there were signs either that his heart was not in his farming, or that farming of the kind that he had embarked on was no longer delivering the means to live the life he had until then led. At that stage, however, there was no external sign of his being beset by financial difficulties. That year was also very close to the start of his remarkable career as a cragsman, and his success in that sphere was on the rise. It may be surmised that there was at least a degree of conflict between the two parts of his life, in terms of the attention that he was giving to each, though there is no evidence that he was aware of any such conflict. His cheerfulness was constantly remarked on throughout his climbing years, and there is no note of his being afflicted by worries in any memoirs either of climbers or indeed of his brother Edmund. Yet, looking ahead to what was to come later, he did have cause for concern about his finances, and it is most unfortunate that there is no historical record of the precise factors that were governing his thinking when he started on a new life as a land agent. All that we have are small scraps of evidence, such as that JWR and his wife took in Oliver Macdonell as a paying guest for a number of years, as noted above. In the light of the evidence we have it might reasonably be assumed that his motive was primarily financial, and that he was in search of additional sources of income.

On 5 October 1899 JWR's mother Elizabeth Robinson died. Her husband was not long to survive the loss and he himself died on December 29 of the same year. The bulk of his property passed to his son John. His daughter Mary Elizabeth was bequeathed the right to reside for her natural life in 'all this house in which I now reside with its appurtenances' – that is, the main house and the outbuildings associated with it. Richard and Edmund received legacies of £800 and £600 respectively.

The legacies were duly paid, and JWR entered on his inheritance. But storm clouds were clearly gathering, of which the taking up of a paid professional career in Keswick was but a harbinger.

JWR was now owner and master of the Whinfell Hall estate. However, he and his wife Janet lived on there, next door to JWR's sister Mary Elizabeth, for only a year, with John going to Keswick to attend to his business as a land agent while continuing to manage the farm. In 1900, a year after the death of his father, came the decision to devote himself entirely to the business at Keswick, and to rent out the farm. What occasioned this decision? JWR may not have wished to afflict his aging parents with bothersome changes at that stage of their lives. Or their eventual death may have made possible a reorganisation of the living space in the two houses. But in any case it seems more than likely that his father and he between them had been failing to make the farm pay.

Already on 10 January 1894 Janet Robinson had written in her circular diary: 'It grieves me to see the lines of care deepening on my dear husband's face. Farming has been bad for years and seems to grow worse', adding wistfully 'But the darkest hour is just before the dawn.' The hours were to get yet darker.

To the general problems that the yeoman farmer was experiencing, noted above, may now be added some factors of more immediate concern. The later 1880s were a time of depression in English agriculture, but the position varied according to locality, yielding a complex picture with many paradoxes. Overall, the key feature of the period was the shift from arable to pastoral farming – from 'corn' to 'horn' – which was to result in the emergence of the Lakeland landscape as we know it today. In this process, Cumbrian farmers on the one hand fared better than elsewhere, and bankruptcies were far fewer than to the south. Much of the Cumbrian farmer's arable production was in any case for consumption and animal feed rather than for sale. What he did produce for the market could now be transported more easily to the industrial periphery on the railways. Some farmers, in favoured places (such as Wasdale Head) could benefit from the growing tourism. On the other hand the change, particularly to cattle rearing, was not an easy one for the small and medium farmer to

Ellerbank in Brigham as it is today

make. Capital outlays were needed for seed and fertilisers, but a major problem was the greater lead time than that required for arable crops.

There was also a marked drop in the labour available. At the time of the 1851 census well over 20 per cent of the occupied population of the Lakes counties worked on the land (against a national figure of nine per cent), but in the following 40 years the number of labourers and indoor servants on farms in Cumbria shrank by almost a half.[2]

Unfortunately we have no detailed record of the impact of these factors in the particular case of the Whinfell Hall holding. It is very clear, however, that JWR was under severe financial pressure as the century drew to a close, sufficient to explain his decision, having rented out the farm and the farmhouse, to move away entirely from the family home, leaving Mary Elizabeth in the main house. In 1900 he rented for himself and his wife a house in Brigham, some five miles from Whinfell Hall, though no nearer to Keswick. This was in fact one half of a semi-detached pair of houses sharing the name of Ellerbank. Then, a year later, on 1 July 1901, he purchased both houses for a total of £650 (see page 119).[3]

To be able to raise that sum without selling any of the Whinfell Hall property might suggest that he was well off at the time. This, however, was far from the case. On 5 February 1900 he had contracted a loan of £1500 from John Brockbank of Aspatria, using the Whinfell Hall property as collateral.[4] Both Whinfell Hall houses were then let, among others to members of the Peile family, which had always been close to the Robinsons.

The Brockbanks were in fact relatives of JWR's mother Elizabeth. John Brockbank and his elder brother had rented a farmstead at Heathfield, near Aspatria, from Sir Wilfrid Lawson and had invested heavily in improving what was regarded locally as a poor piece of land. Edmund describes in his correspondence how the Brockbanks hauled tons of stable manure and further tons of artificial fertiliser as that came onto the market in order to improve both his pasturage and his corn crops. They were so successful that when a law was brought in to make landlords pay compensation for improvements, Sir Wilfrid was loath to pay the large sum that the Brockbanks' enterprise had earned, and he preferred to sell them the holding. Here was a yeoman family bucking the trend of decline of that class, but doing so by drawing the right conclusions from the direction of agricultural change and by investing for longer term returns than those offered by largely arable crops.

At all events, that John Brockbank had surplus to lend while JWR had to borrow suggests that in the latter's affairs something more was going on than could be accounted for by the difficulties of yeoman farming. It became even clearer that his financial difficulties were deepening in 1903, when he contracted a further loan of £600, this time from John Musgrave, whose estate he was managing at the time. Later, on 8 October 1906, Musgrave was in addition to take over the balance of the 1900 mortgage. Neither loan was ever to be repaid, though it appears that JWR was able to cope with the interest on them. Whatever fee Musgrave was paying him for managing his estate was returning as interest on the loan to a man who must certainly on balance be reckoned a benefactor to JWR.

It is not clear exactly when JWR took to speculating on the stock market. In principle there was nothing special about yeoman farmers investing the surplus of their farming efforts in financial speculation. Even in the eighteenth century they had invested along with merchants, shopkeepers and tradesmen in the growing ports of the Cumbrian coasts. On the other hand we have no record of JWR's engaging in stock-market speculation before the turn of the century, when he was investing heavily in South African mines. Moreover, when his affairs were being sorted out after his death in 1907, there were share certificates only from that sector. At all events, by 1905 he was not only heavily involved in activity on the stock market, but was faring very badly.

For one whose grip on money matters was apparently never too firm, and at a time when the farming interest in the Lake District was undergoing change, the opportunity must have seemed golden. More than one eye was glittering at the opening of the mining industry in South Africa. The discovery of diamonds at Kimberley in 1870 and of large gold deposits in the Witwatersrand region of the Transvaal in 1886 had caused an influx of European (mainly British) immigration and investment. By 1898 South Africa was the leading producer, and production was set to become far higher. Then came the Boer War, the British victory in which made speculation even more attractive. JWR joined the rush.

That JWR, the cheery Quaker pioneer of rock-climbing and Cumbrian dalesman, should be turning to speculation in this way, with all the risks it involved, is surprising, and conflicts with the 'Nestor' image that he had acquired in his approach to rock-climbing. It can only be interpreted as an anxious, possibly desperate, search for ways of solving his financial difficulties. Equally surprising is the fact that he appears to have been fully familiar not only with the world of share dealing but also with the technicalities of mining in South Africa. This may have been transmitted to him by a particular friend, who is known in JWR's correspondence simply as Albert, and whom at one point he calls his 'guide'. Albert was an engineer who went in and out of South Africa in the years around and during the Boer War, doing deals in which he from J. W. Robinson

Keswick
April 9th '05

My dear Richard

I have received your letter, containing particulars of the cash owing to thee by the company. I sent it in on Saturday to Waugh & Musgrave and told them I would call early this week as I would not be in Cockermouth today. They will make enquiry and advise as to what can be done. My hope is that these directors here will not want the blown up. Be sure if you move to arrange for all letters to be forwarded to you. As to your money, you must be sure and let me know if you do want more. I want to tell you fully all about my connection with African mines. Your plan to sell half is just what I ought to have done and I should have taken no harm but losing my guide his going back to South Africa was a bad thing for me. Well to begin with the brothers Hooper both Mining Engineers were in Africa when war broke out and there they stayed. George the older was at

A page of the letter from JWR to his brother Richard,
dated 9 April, 1905.

involved JWR, but also using JWR as his agent in England. In a letter to his brother Richard in the United States of 9 April 1905 JWR writes that Albert:

showed me how low mines were and what were the prospects of a boom. He and I invested all we had and also contracted loans at the Bank. We did too well. I had at one time a profit of £1500 and I ought to have cleared out and cleared off the mortgage on Whinfell Hall. But this idea of a big big boom was strong upon us and we thought of all the development that the Big Houses who Enginier all Booms wanted to do. Then came the labour trouble and things went down and down.[5]

Later in the same letter he writes, 'I think if I can hold on for 12 months and a big rise comes I shall not be quite ruined as I at one time this spring thought I was'. It appears that he was led by what he calls the Big Houses to overstretch himself, with disastrous results.

Presumably through his personal connection with Albert, an engineer, JWR followed closely the mining activities that his speculation depended upon, down to detailed calculations of the depth to which the East Rand Deep mine should bore in order to strike the reef it was seeking. All these matters, financial and technical, he retailed in his correspondence with his brother Richard who, it seems, at one point considered moving from the United States to South Africa, and who gave JWR advice which his brother did not always heed: 'Your plan to sell half is just what I ought to have done and I should have taken no harm', writes JWR at one point.

JWR's other brother, Edmund, wrote in a letter to his friend John Walker of Saffron Walden:

That kind of investment is very closely akin to gambling, indeed it is often difficult to draw the line in such investments between legitimate investment and gambling. But ... he was led into a course from which retreat was almost impossible. We [ourselves] did not lose anything, as he had paid up [what he owed us], but he did lose some (the most, except for the percentage prepaid, half I think) of Richard's. John was not entirely to blame. He raised the money to pay him off, as he did for me, and put it in the bank, but could get no reply from R. as to what to do with it. Then he tried to borrow it, and getting no reply borrowed it anyway. Richard got his letters and should have written.

In the same letter Edmund continues 'John lost some of Mary's [money] too, but not so much as for Richard. I think he put up some of her stock as security on a loan without due authority. I suppose it was done in the extremity, hoping to recuperate'.

The question inevitably arises whether JWR's effective loss of the Whinfell Hall houses and the financial difficulties that ended in very unwise speculation in African mines put pressures on him that contributed to the deterioration of his health and his early death at the age of 54. We know from his letter to Richard, just cited, that this was the view of his wife Janet. Certainly he must have had more than his share of worry at the time. The cheerful face he turned towards his rock-climbing companions may have been a way of escaping from the miseries in one department of his life into the marked successes in another – if, indeed, that escaping was not another factor contributing to his lack of success in making the farm pay.

1 Records of Waugh & Musgrave, Solicitors, CRO, Whitehaven.
2 Marshall, J.D. and J.K. Walton, *The Lake Counties from 1830 to the Mid-Twentieth Century*, Manchester: Manchester University Press, 1981, Appendix 4.
3 Deeds of Ellerbank, now 14, High Brigham, courtesy of Dennis Hinde.
4 Deeds of Whinfell Hall.
5 I am grateful to Polly Jones, Edmund Robinson's great-grandniece, for providing me with copies of this correspondence.

Chapter 9:
The Final Phase

We have no record of JWR's thoughts and feelings during these difficult years. The few letters that have survived concern his speculation in African mining, and they are mostly of a practical nature. Janet and he left no posterity to transmit the personal details of the closing years of his life. The move to Brigham must have been a wrench, associated as it was with the mortgaging of the Whinfell Hall houses and land. Little noticed in the climbing literature is the lacuna in his activity on the rocks in the early years of the dawning twentieth century. From 1884 onwards his Diary shows him making a number of ascents of his beloved Pillar Rock each year, though in some years as few as two. One of those years is 1900. In the preceding year he made only a single ascent, and likewise in 1901. Then there is a gap until 1905 with no ascents at all. He is climbing Pillar again in 1906, when he made his 100th and 101st ascents. But by then he was clearly experiencing problems with his health, no less than with his finances. It was in that year that crisis struck, and it is a pity that we have no clue to his – or Janet's – inner feelings at the time.

In August 1906 a group of climbing colleagues set off with JWR to make his hundredth ascent of Pillar Rock. George Seatree, who was in the group, maintained later that JWR was not quite himself on this occasion. Later, on the last Sunday of September 1906, JWR set off for Deep Ghyll on Scafell with two companions, George Muller and J.A.Carter. One of them records how it was a clear, warm, sunny day. JWR was his usually gay jesting self, but now and then would fall into an uncharacteristic reverie. When they reached the Keswick Brothers climb, JWR announced that the moment was not propitious, and led the party off to finish the day on simpler climbs. The chronicler ends his account:

The sun went down in splendour into the Irish Sea. Heliotrope on the mountains turned to ebony. As we came down Brown Tongue a chill wind got up. The weather was changing. Next day was cold and wet. We were in for one of the clashiest and clartiest back-ends for years. John never climbed again.

George Seatree takes up the tale in his 'In memoriam', published in the *Fell and Rock Climbing Club Journal* after JWR's death. On 15 May 1907 Seatree had a letter from JWR telling him: 'I have an internal ailment which I hope to overcome, but it is quite impossible for me to climb this summer, in consequence, I may not cycle much or walk much'. The ailment was in fact an incipient cancer in the gut, which became acute in the early part of the summer. It was hoped that a holiday might restore his health, and JWR went with his wife to her family's house in Yorkshire. After a short time they went for a second holiday on the Isle of Man. But later in the summer the crisis came, and it was decided that he should undergo an operation. It was successful, but JWR was too weak to recover from it and he died on 20 August 1907.

He was buried in the simple burying ground of the Friends' Meeting House in Pardshaw, which he had attended all his life. The interment took place at 4.15 p.m. on 23 August 1907. Already there were six family graves in the burial ground, those of Wilson Robinson the elder and his wife Jane, JWR's grandmother Mary Sutton, and JWR's siblings who had died in infancy or youth - Jane, Emily and Arthur.

The members of the newly formed Fell and Rock Climbing Club were naturally dismayed by the disappearance, so early in its existence, of one of the Club's most cherished members, and its Vice-Chairman to boot. The Club's Journal records how, at a meeting of its Committee held in Ulverston on 25 September 1907, the following motion was carried 'in ominous silence':

That this Committee has received the intelligence of the death of Mr. John Wilson Robinson, the senior Vice-President of the Club, with the deepest sorrow, and records its keen sense of the great loss which the Club, mountaineers generally, and the whole community have sustained by the sad event.

It was decided that a memorial to JWR be erected, and a sub-committee was set up to make the appropriate arrangements, containing 13 members of the Club who were personally close to the deceased dalesman, and who were the flower of the rock-climbing fraternity in the English Lake District. When the Memorial Committee met in Manchester on October 19 it was chaired by Charles Pilkington, J.P. of Manchester,

The Robinson Cairn
*The cairn was built after JWR's death to commemorate his contribution
to rock-climbing in the Lake district. It is situated on the High-Level route
from the Black Sail Pass to Pillar Rock, pioneered by JWR. The figure in
the photograph is Haskett-Smith, who led the construction of the cairn*

not a member of the first nominated group, but someone capable of drawing in further notable public figures to promote the creation of a fund on a broad geographical base. Six such figures were added to the Committee at that meeting, listed in the Fell and Rock Climbing Club's minutes (in addition to Charles Pilkington) in the following form:

Sir Wilfrid Lawson, Bart., Cumberland
Canon H.D.Rawnsley, M.A., Keswick
Principal Hopkinson, Manchester
Prof. Procter, Leeds
George B.Bryant, Esq., London
W.W.Naismith, Esq., Glasgow

The maximum subscription was fixed at five shillings, and a circular inviting people to subscribe was sent to the various other climbing clubs.

After a number of meetings in Manchester it was agreed that a bronze tablet be appropriately inscribed and affixed to the rock at the end of the High Level route to Pillar Rock which JWR had himself pioneered. Reservations were expressed on the grounds that the memorial might create an awkward precedent, but they were overcome in view of JWR's very special standing. In association with this proposal, a group of JWR's old friends, together with members of the Alpine, Climbers, Yorkshire Ramblers, Fell and Rock and other climbing clubs, went up to the site on Easter Saturday 1908 and built a cairn near where the tablet was to be mounted. Walter Haskett-Smith directed the proceedings. The 'Robinson Cairn' still today serves as a marker to the location of the tablet.

The tablet could not be mounted on the same day, as originally planned, because the casting was not ready, and the ceremony was postponed until Whitsun. Unfortunately, this date, too, failed, the Chairman of the Committee being unable to attend. Finally, the date for mounting the tablet was fixed at June 13, and the ceremony was duly held on that day, despite the Chairman's yet again being unable to attend. His place was taken by Cecil Slingsby, another old friend and climbing companion of the deceased cragsman.

On the evening of June 12, Slingsby, George Seatree and George Müller gathered at the Angler's Inn in Ennerdale, together with the contractor, Mr Benson Walker, and his associates. The evening was fine, and all augured well for the morrow. The Lake District weather, however,

The memorial tablet to John Wilson Robinson.

even in June, is used to frustrating the best laid of plans, and during the night a storm blew up, driven by a severe gale from the west. Mr Walker set off early with his men, dragging the heavy tablet and their gear. The rest of the party followed later and were joined near Gillerthwaite Farm by L.J.Oppenheimer, who had made his way with difficulty over Scarth Gap. The storm was reaching its apogee as they arrived at the High Level route, and it was clear that the tablet was not to be mounted that day. It was left leaning on the rock, and the small group huddled in the scanty shelter that could be found to hear a speech shouted into the wind by Cecil Slingsby. The words of the speech are given in the Appendix of this book.

The record of these events can be found in the *Fell and Rock Climbing Club Journal*, which continues with a description of the downward journey.[2] Pillar Rock itself was almost beyond recognition. The great bastion appeared to be hung with garlands of lace, the well-known gully climbs on the north face being transformed into foaming cataracts. The rills were swollen into heavy streams, the streams into rivers. The Lisa … was in mad impassable state … Through blinding sheets of rain, the storm-driven travellers trudged and waded up the bleak valley to the Black Sail footbridge, which at first looked to have been washed away, but ultimately the plank was found several feet under water.

The storm, having made its contribution to the solemnity of the occasion, abated towards evening. The next day dawned fine, and the party was able to visit JWR's old home at Whinfell Hall to round off their tribute to their departed friend in an atmosphere of serenity.

* * *

On the Monday following, Mr Walker completed the mounting of the tablet. The inscription on it reads as follows:

FOR REMEMBRANCE OF
JOHN WILSON ROBINSON,
OF WHINFELL HALL, IN LORTON,
WHO DIED 1907, AT BRIGHAM.
ONE HUNDRED OF HIS COMRADES
AND FRIENDS RAISED THIS.
HE KNEW AND LOVED AS NONE OTHER
THESE HIS NATIVE CRAGS AND FELLS,
WHENCE HE DREW
SIMPLICITY, STRENGTH AND CHARM.
'WE CLIMB THE HILL: FROM END TO END
IN ALL THE LANDSCAPE UNDERNEATH
WE FIND NO PLACE THAT DOES NOT BREATHE
SOME GRACIOUS MEMORY OF OUR FRIEND.'

The concluding stanza will be recognised as being drawn from Tennyson's poem *In Memoriam*, written after the death of his closest friend, Arthur Hallam, in 1833. Tennyson's 'I' had been replaced with a collective 'we' (the 'in' for the poet's 'of' presumably being an error that crept in during the process of transcription).

The party had also taken with them onto the Rock a bottle, encased

130

in an enamelled zinc box, and containing a 'Record of Memorial' written on parchment. This was to have been placed in the cairn by the tablet, but the conditions rendered this, too, impracticable. It was put there finally in August, during a meet of the Club. The text can be found in the Appendix, accompanying Cecil Slingsby's speech of 1 June.

For the record, the amount subscribed to the Memorial Fund was £40 15s. 9d. The cost of the tablet, including inscription and mounting, came to £28 5s. 3d. The balance was transferred to a 'Private Relief Fund', which the Committee decided to promote.

JWR's wife Janet had to leave the Brigham house when JWR's affairs were wound up. She writes in her circular diary to her former pupils in November 1908: 'I am quite in the dark as to where my next abiding place is to be – or what my work. But I am finding how the cultivation of absolute trust in the Divine guidance pays…I am sure there is work yet for me to do – "something e'er the end – some work of noble note may yet be done"'. After this black moment of doubt qualified by hope she went back to Shipley to live with the family from which she had come. She died in Shipley on 9 February 1931, aged 80, but her grave is in the burial ground of the Pardshaw Meeting House next to that of her husband. It was the end of a life about which we know little, but which must have had more than its share of anxieties. The couple died childless, and so she had been denied the company of children during JWR's life and their comfort after his death.

Mary Elizabeth lived to the age of 78, remaining single until she was 56. On 17 December 1907, almost immediately after JWR's death, she married Alexander Dunlop in the Friends' Meeting House at Carlisle and thereafter lived with him at Mountain View in Cockermouth until her death in 1928. In the opinion of Mary's brother Edmund, this Alexander Dunlop was a 'bad lot'. The cottage at Mountain View had been left to Mary Elizabeth by Mary Robinson of Eaglesfield, and apparently Dunlop obliged Mary Elizabeth to bequeath it to him.[3] Moreover, he refused to allow her to associate with her old friends (the Harris family of Derwent Bank is specifically mentioned), nor would he let JWR's wife Janet into the house. According to Edmund, a Dunlop relative said of Alexander that he had seen off three wives. This time, Alexander said, he was marrying

131

John Wilson Robinson's gravestone

a rich woman. 'In which he was fooled', notes Edmund. We know, however, that Mary was bequeathed £400 on JWR's death as her interest in Whinfell Hall which, whilst it would not constitute a substantial fortune, was not a negligible sum at the time. The sum was presumably paid, if indeed it was paid in full at all, from the sale of Whinfell Hall which necessarily ensued, given the extent of JWR's indebtedness. According to his Will, proved in Carlisle on 15 May 1908, his wife Janet inherited the residue of his estate.

When JWR died there was a balance of £104.9s.11d. in his account at the London City and Midland Bank in Cockermouth. The full sum of £2,100 raised by mortgaging his major asset, Whinfell Hall with its two houses and land, remained unpaid. The Brigham house, on the other hand, was unencumbered. This was let for a short while and then on 15 June 1908 was sold to a Joseph Harrison for a price of £650. Shares in a number of concerns, many of them in mining, were left. A dividend on £274.0s.0d. of stock in the London and North-West Railway was paid to

Robinson graves in the burial ground of the Pardshaw
Friends' Meeting House

his executor after his death.[4] We know that when he died he had holdings in Kafir Tins Development Co., Central South African Lands and Mines, the 'Athena' Gold Mining and Development Co., and Monastery Diamond Mines and Estates, but we do not know what the sale of these fetched. His executors had difficulty in finding an acceptable price for a bunch of other shares, this time in the Coronation Syndicate, East Rand Extension Gold, and Piggs Peak Development Co., valued at £94.13s.8., £47.10s.0d. and £35.12s.6d. respectively.

On 27 July 1908 a certain R J Holdsworth paid a deposit of £420 for the purchase of the entire Whinfell Hall property, and the rest of a total price of £4,200 on November 9. Of that sum, £2100 (more precisely £2121.18s.11d.) went in repaying the debt owing to John Musgrave. Eight days later Mary Elizabeth Dunlop was paid her £400 for her interest in Whinfell Hall, the overall balance then passing to Janet, JWR's widow. It was in this way that Whinfall Hall, first brought together by John Wilson in 1734 as a consolidated holding, passed from the family's tenure and then ownership. At least JWR was spared the pain of living through this final dénouement, but it was none the less he who, in his brother Edmund's words, had 'lost the houses'. Edmund's descendants in the United States have never forgiven JWR for that.

Most of JWR's effects were sold at auction by Mitchell's in Cockermouth. They raised £140.5s.11d. for house furniture and £6.8s.0d. for his office furniture and work tools.

* * *

In moving towards an assessment of the life of JWR, with its various facets, it must be asked what led this nature-lover from simply going about on foot among the fells to taking part in a sport whose competitive nature and raised levels of accepted risk conflicted at least to some extent with his habits, knowledge, and respect for the rocks. His friendship with people like George Seatree must count for much. Seatree was a Cumbrian, like JWR, but he enters history as a climber without the naturalist background of JWR, and his role in drawing JWR to the rocks must have been important. Also influential, it may be surmised, was a subdued competitiveness in JWR which, though held in check by his upbringing, did in fact attract him to that aspect of the sport of climbing. But the decisive influence must surely have been the arrival on his Lakeland scene of the visitors to Wasdale Head. It did not take long for him to discover a commonality of interests with them and for both parties to realise that they had much to teach each other.

There were, therefore, a number of factors leading him towards his career as a cragsman. Yet the motivations of the Wasdale visitors were after all somewhat different from his. It is clear that the affection that they had for him and the respect in which they held him were perfectly sincere, but these attitudes were articulated — through comments made and through the very behaviour of the visitors towards him — in ways that reveal a distance between him and them, a sense that what they had in common was real enough, but did not englobe the whole of the mutual relationship. In the words cited above of a family friend, and not a visitor: 'Why was J.W.R. so beloved?... Why is it that his name, that so ordinary surname, mentioned among climbers who have known him brings such a whirl of recollections, tough climbs, jokes, fell walks before them and something else too?' The 'something else' that JWR contributed was

134

partly personal, and partly the product of JWR's cultural roots as a Cumbrian yeoman farmer who was also a Quaker. The personal and the cultural come together in his concern over accidents and incurring unnecessary dangers, which ran counter to an ethos of the winning of accolades at the expense of risk.

It might be asked, then, whether JWR would have taken to the rocks if he had not made the acquaintance of these people injected into his Lakeland space. The question, however, is hardly worth pursuing. What is important is the 'being there' factor. It was JWR's destiny to have been in his physical prime, with a deep knowledge of the fells, and with an expansive personality that invited partnership, at the particular historical moment when the sport of rock-climbing arrived in the English Lake District. This simple fact of 'being there' outweighs all questions of personal motivation, powerful though these were.

The information contained in these pages will, it is hoped, go some way also to answering some questions of no immediate concern to climbers, including whether his climbing activities undermined to any extent his personal life, and contributed to the ultimate loss of Whinfell Hall. A comment on JWR made by one of his companions on the rocks is revealing: 'On the fells John was a boy not grown up. He infected everybody with his merry spirit. He was the life and soul of every party. He was a great man'.[5] Was he in fact in some sense 'not grown up'? There is a charge of irresponsibility hanging over him in the family's later collective memory, countering the climbing fraternity's universally positive evaluation of his life. In the image transmitted down the years to Edmund's family today he was a gambler. His prominent place in the history of climbing in the English Lake District is secure. To what extent was this prominence vitiated by failings in his life away from the rocks?

Unfortunately the evidence that we have does not allow us to come to a firm conclusion on this question. We do know that the circumstances of his time were pressing hard on the class of yeomen farmers. There were objective factors that could explain his financial difficulties quite independently of the expenditure of time that his climbing activities imposed. The same objective factors could explain his speculation in South African mining and lessen any opprobrium attaching to him as a result of its apparently disastrous outcome.

It could also be asked whether his close association with these often distinguished and highly educated 'off-comers' who had arrived so abruptly on his patch might have affected his attitude to his own means of making a living, devaluing it and reducing his concentration on matters that had a prior claim on his attention as a farmer. But he seems to have been able to cope remarkably well with that association over a long period.

At this personal level it is perhaps fairest to conclude simply that the times were against him as a gentleman farmer. Not only his walking and climbing, but also his quite extensive involvement in local affairs, were losing their economic supports. If, as family opinion has it, he was not good with money, this would only have aggravated a problem that was already facing his class when he took charge of the Whinfell Hall farm holding.

In sum, he was a man of his time. This had both negative and positive aspects. In the historical record, his particular individual contribution to the sport of rock-climbing in the Lake District, described in the first part of this book, has given him a deserved prominence. In the story of the decline of the Lakeland yeoman farmer, on the other hand, no claim to individuality on the historical scene can be made for him. His fate here merges with that of the other members of his class. The aim of this book has been to rescue from the unread pages of history sufficient detail to endow an idiosyncratic but important mountaineer with a personal historical profile.

* * *

By 1957, when the farmhouse, the cottage and all the land beyond the main house's extensive garden were sold off, the agricultural scene had been transformed out of all recognition. The purchasing farmer, like most of his Lakeland peers by that date, was to make an uncomfortably small living out of sheep and a few cattle. His son was to find a better future by opening a caravan site removed from the houses, with camping permitted on a field adjoining the farmhouse. What has in the above been termed the 'main house' retained the name of Whinfell Hall. It is there that these words are being written, words intended to recapture the yeoman's life that JWR lived, and to fill in hitherto unknown corners of the biography of a remarkable Lakeland climbing pioneer.

1 'A Founder Member' (anon., but presumed to be George Muller), 'Memories of John Wilson Robinson', *Fell and Rock Climbing Club Journal*, 14:3, 1946, pp.208-210.

2 *Fell and Rock Climbing Club Journal*, 1:2, 1908, pp.126-31. The Minute is unsigned but bears all the marks of authorship by George Seatree, the Club's Secretary and Treasurer.

3 *Extracts from Letters Written by Edmund Robinson late of Whinfell Hall to J.G.Brooker 1931-1943*, typescript, held in the archive of the Lorton and Derwent Fells Local History Society, pp.43 and 53.

4 Records of Waugh & Musgrave, Solicitors, CRO, Whitehaven.

5 'A Founder Member', 'Memories of John Wilson Robinson', *Fell and Rock Climbing Club Journal*, 14:3, 1946, p.210.

Appendix 1

Cecil Slingsby's speech on the occasion of the erection of the memorial to John Wilson Robinson on Pillar Rock on 13 June 1908.

We are assembled here to assist in the erection of a memorial of very especial interest. We are drawn together from the north, from the south, from the east and from the west—all imbued with one common feeling, the deep love and admiration of dear old John Robinson. Owing mainly to the uncertainty of the date when the bronze tablet would be ready, we were unable to arrange for it to be fixed on the day originally intended, namely, the Saturday before Whit Sunday, and hence to-day was chosen. This change has, I regret to say, prevented many very old friends of Robinson's being present, whose absence we much regret. Notably is this the case with Mr. Haskett-Smith, the great pioneer of the modern type of rock-climbing in Cumberland, and who undoubtedly was Robinson's chief mountaineering companion. There are many others who would have liked to be present to-day. Fortunately, one of the oldest friends, tried and true, Seatree, is with us, and to him is due the thanks of us all for the energy, skill, and tact which he has used upon a true labour of love, the result of which we now all see before us.

Just a few words about mountaineering with dear old John. A great theme it is, too, and one in which are interwoven many most delightful recollections. To know Robinson was to love him. To climb with him, whether in sunshine or in storm, was always a keen enjoyment. His sunny nature and almost universal optimism were delightful characteristics. No matter how tired and hungry we were, how heavily the pitiless rain, how thick the clouds, how fierce the wind, how trying the cold, how near to great success had been our failure, if Robinson were with us the time passed pleasantly away, and it was impossible to be dull.

John's brightness and jollity were positively infectious. He was always full of fun, ready to make a joke and enjoy it too. Well do we all remember his hearty laugh. His memory was marvellous, especially in recalling minute details, which, though full of interest, we had all forgotten. As a mountaineer he was in every respect first-rate, and had that rare gift of being able to read a mountain like a book. He was a magnificent route finder. No one had such a marvellous knowledge of the details of the Cumberland fells as he. Like all good mountaineers he loved the mountains with an intense love and a wholesome respect. He was bold as a lion, but took no unwarrantable risks, as he possessed the great moral courage of being able to sound a retreat when experience dictated that to advance would be to court danger. Many a time have I climbed with Robinson and rejoiced with success or laughed at failure. Robinson, with Haskett-Smith, Hastings, Charles Hopkinson, and myself, did much of the exploratory work on the north face of the Pillar Rock, a much more difficult matter than is generally supposed. Unfortunately when success smiled upon us he was unable to join the party. This was much regretted by all. He, however, made the second ascent. He was in the first unsuccessful attempt to ascend Moss Ghyll, and I shall never forget the way which he climbed the mossy wall of rock up to the Tennis Court Ledge: as fine a bit of climbing as I have ever seen. This wall is much changed now. Fortunately John was one of the party in the successful ascent when 'the Collie Step' was cut. This was not my luck.

A true ladies' man was our dear old friend in the best sense of the word, and many a winsome lassie has he introduced to the heart of the fells and to the best climbs in Lakeland. Not only did he lead them up, but also on several occasions he descended with one or more ladies the grimmest rock faces in Cumberland, a much more severe achievement, and a phase of British mountaineering which is too much neglected. Our dear old friend possessed in a high degree all the best characteristics of the north country yeoman, the back-bone of our race. In many cases, and most certainly in that of Robinson, these northern yeomen are the descendants of the Norse 'bonder'. John Robinson was essentially of Scandinavian ancestry, and I have often called him a British Norseman. If I could have paid him a higher compliment I would have done so. Though the hand of death has led our dear friend to his long sleep, all who, like myself, have enjoyed for many years his friendship and close comradeship on the fells of his native county will have a rich store of happy memories of John Robinson, which we shall cherish as a precious possession so long as life shall last.

Appendix 2

The text of the parchment placed in a bottle and deposited on the Robinson cairn on Pillar Rock in August 1908.

RECORD OF MEMORIAL
In memory of John Wilson Robinson, born at Whinfell Hall, Lorton, 1853; died at Brigham 1907. An enthusiastic and skilful cragsman, who, between the years 1882 and 1906 ascended this rock by various routes over 100 times. A true lover of nature, and one of nature's own gentlemen, John Wilson Robinson endeared himself to a wide circle of mountaineering friends, who retain the keenest appreciation of his many kind acts and his genial and friendly intercourse during their visits to the Cumberland fells. At Easter this year a cairn was erected to his memory by a few friends on a knoll by the side of the High Level route to Black Sail Pass. On a face of rock near to the cairn, which may henceforth be known as Robinson's cairn, has been fixed, on this 13th day of June, 1908, a bronze memorial tablet, subscribed for by over one hundred of his comrades and friends, who thus desire to perpetuate his memory.

Signed and deposited here on behalf of the Memorial Committee, whose names are given below,

GEORGE SEATREE
Hon. Secretary and Treasurer

W.P.HASKETT-SMITH (Chairman), G.D.ABRAHAM, WALTER BRUNSKILL, G.B.BRYANT, PROFESSOR J.NORMAN COLLIE, GEOFFREY HASTINGS, ALFRED HOPKINSON, K.C., F.W.JACKSON, G.W.MÜLLER, W.W.NAISMITH, L.J.OPPENHEIMER, C.PILKINGTON, PROFESSOR PROCTER, E.H.P.SCANTLEBURY, WILLIAM CECIL SLINGSBY, PROFESSOR WILBERFORCE, C.N.WILLIAMSON

Appendix 3

*The objects of the and Rock Climbing Club, as summarised in 'The Origins and Aims of our Club', and printed in the **Fell and Rock Climbing Club Journal**, Vol.1, No.1, pp.13-14.*

1. To encourage and foster under the safest and most helpful conditions the exhilarating exercise and sport of Fell Rambling and Rock Climbing in the Lake District.

2. To serve as an instrument of union, and to promote friendship and comradery amongst lovers of mountaineering, either visiting or residing in the District and near it.

3. To arrange for periodical ' Meets' of the members of the Club and their friends in order that they may participate in either form of mountain pastime, and become a sure source of mutual aid and encouragement.

4. To provide at the Club centres or other convenient points, suitable mountaineering literature, guide-books, maps, ropes, etc. To adopt means for members obtaining the best information as to local accommodation, and all other matters pertaining to the adjacent fells.

5. To provide a Climbing Book for the use of members only, at each of the five principal Club Centres, viz. Wastdale, Coniston, Langdale, Rosthwaite, and Buttermere. These books will be provided for members to record descriptions of ascents, notable experiences, excursions on the Fells, and suggestions for the Committee. Members and custodians are requested to guard these volumes as much as possible from all improper usage.

6. A Membership Ticket will be issued on payment of subscription. This ticket must be produced when applying to the Hotel Proprietors at the different Centres for the use of the Club's Books, Ropes, etc.

7. The Committee intend eventually to arrange for Lectures, the publishing of a Journal or Annual, the founding of a Library, the collection of Mountain Photographs and Lantern Slides, and in all respects to study and further the interests of the growing community of Mountaineers frequenting the area of the Club's operations.

Appendix 4

John Wilson Robinson's Participation in First Ascents

Date	Climb	Other participants
1884, Sept.1	Needle Ridge	Haskett-Smith
1884, Sept. 20	Scafell Pinnacle by Steep Ghyll, Low Man and High Man	Haskett-Smith
1886	E Buttress, Dow Crag	Haskett-Smith
1889	Green Crag Gully	W.A.Wilson
1890, Dec. 29	Shamrock Gully	G.Hastings, C. Hopkinson
1892, April 20	Second pitch of Deep Ghyll (known as Robinson's chimney)	O.G.Jones and others
1892, Dec. 26	Moss Ghyll	J.N.Collie, G.Hastings
1892, Dec. 27	Great Gully, The Screes	G.Hastings, J.N.Collie
1893	Black Chimney on Chapel Crags (High Style)	O.G.Jones
1893	Central Chimney on Chapel Crags	O.G.Jones, W.A.Wilson
1893 Sept. 1	Raven Crag Gully	W.A.Wilson
1893, Sept. 6	Sergeant Crag Gully	O.G.Jones
1893, Dec.26	Kern Knotts Chimney and The Crack	O.G.Jones, W.H.Fowler
1894, Sept.23	Shamrock Chimney	R.S.R., L.R.Wilberforce, W.H.Price
1896, June	Iron Crag Chimney	G.Abraham, F.W.Jackson
1898, Sept. 10	West Wall Climb on Scafell	T.H.Doncaster, H.W.Blunt

Information from Fell and Rock Climbing Club's Journal and guide books

A note on sources

Numbered references in this book have been kept to a minimum, and are re-stricted chiefly to works that themselves are referenced (which is rarely the case in the climbing literature), and to cases where it is not clear to which of a given author's works reference is being made. The sources are organised below in a way that will lead the reader to the works consulted, the names of authors having been systematically inserted in the text. Some titles have been added to give a more comprehensive list for the interested reader.

Abbreviations used:
CRO   Cumbria Record Office
FRCCJ   Fell and Rock Climbing Club Journal

Original Sources
JWR's own writings were few, but include 'A novice in the snow', FRCCJ, 1:1 (1907); 'Camping amongst the crags in 1885', FRCCJ 4:2 (1917-18); and his words in Rumney, A.W, 'John Wilson Robinson's walk , FRCCJ, 3:3 (1915). Records of his talks to local societies can be found in his Scrapbook in the CRO at Kendal. His climbing diary can also be found there, as can rare entries by him in the Wasdale Hotel Visitors' Book.
A circular diary kept by Janet Wilson and some of her former pupils, The Budget, is kept by the archive of Sidcot School, Winscombe, Somerset. The novel Thorston Hall, by O.S.Macdonell, was published in London by Selwyn & Blount, 1936.
Edmund Robinson's memoirs are in Extracts from Letters Written by Edmund Robinson late of Whinfell Hall to J.G.Brooker 1931-1943, and Extracts from Letters Written by Edmund Robinson late of Whinfell Hall to J.G.Brooker from 1942 and other notes, typescript, held in the archive of the Lorton and Derwent Fells Local History Society.
The Bowring Papers: Diaries of Frederick Herman Bowring can be found at the John Rylands University Library, Manchester (English MSS 1232), various dates.

The chief works cited on **the Lake District and its social history** are:
Baron, Michael G. and Derek Denman, Wordsworth and the Famous Yew Tree, Lorton and Derwent Fells Local History Society, 2004.
Bouch, C.M.L.and G.P.Jones, A Social and Economic History of the Lake Counties 1500-1830, Manchester, 1961.

Bradbury, J.B., *A History of Cockermouth,* Chichester: Phillimore, 1981.

Brailsford, Dennis, *British Sport – A Social History,* Cambridge UK and Maryland MA: Lutterworth and Barnes & Noble, 1992

Brunskill, R.W., *Vernacular Architecture of the Lake Counties,* London and Boston: Faber and Faber, 1974

Butler, David M., *Quaker Meeting-Houses in the Lake Counties,* London and Philadelphia PE: Friends Historical Society, 1978.

Head, Walter, 'Manorial records', *Lorton and Derwent Fells Local History Society Newsletter,* No.35, May 2005.

Lowerson, John, *Sport and the English Middle Classes, 1870-1914,* Manchester and New York NY : Manchester University Press, 1993.

Marshall, J. D. and J.K.Walton, *The Lake Counties from 1830 to the Mid-Twentieth Century,* Manchester: Manchester University Press, 1981, p.191.

Nicholson, Norman, *The Lakers,* London: Robert Hale, 1955.

Rollinson, William, *A History of Man in the Lake District,* London: Dent, 1967.

Winchester, A.J.L., *Landscape and Society in Medieval Cumbria,* Edinburgh: John Donald, 1987.

The following articles concerning JWR have appeared in the ***Fell and Rock Climbing Club Journal:***

'*A Founder Member*', 'Memories of John Wilson Robinson', 14:3 (1946)

Anon., 'The Memorial to the late J.W.Robinson', 1:2 (1908).

Bott, George, 'A pride of Robinsons', 20:3 (1966).

Hall, Richard, 'A paper on J.W.Robinson for the members of the F.R.C.C.', 5:1 (1919)

Haskett-Smith, W.P., 'Doe Crag and John Robinson', 1:3 (1909).

Seatree George, 'In Memoriam – John W. Robinson', 1:1 (1907).

Seatree, George, 'Reminiscences of early Lakeland mountaineering', 2:1 (1910).

The following are the works on ***rock-climbing in the English Lake District*** cited in the text, with additions to provide a slim basic bibliography on the topic:

Abraham, George D, *British Mountain Climbs,* London: Mills and Boon, 1923.

Birkett, Bill, *Lakeland's Greatest Pioneers*, London: Robert Hale, 1983

Griffin, A.H., *Inside the Real Lake District,* Preston: The Guardian Press, 1961.

Hankinson, Alan, *A Century on the Crags: The Story of Rock-Climbing in the English Lake District*, Striding Edge, 1997.

Hankinson, Alan, *The First Tigers,* Bassenthwaite: Melbeck, 1972, revised 1984.

Haskett-Smith,W.P. *Climbing in the British Isles*, London: Longman, 1894; facsimile Ernest Press, 1956.

Jones, O.G., *Rock-Climbing in the English Lake District,* Manchester: E.J.Morten, 1973.

Jones, T., and G. Milburn, *Cumbrian Rock,* Glossop: Pic Publications, 1988.

Kelly H.M. and W. Peascod, *Rock-Climbing Guides to the English Lake District: Pillar Rock and Neighbourhood,* revised edition, Stockport: Fell and Rock Climbing Club, 1952.

Kelly, H.M. and J.H.Doughty, 'A short history of Lakeland climbing: Part I (1802-1934)', *FRCCJ,* Lakeland Number, 1936-7.

Lefebure, Molly, *The English Lake District,* New York: Hastings House, 1964.

Oppenheimer, L.J., *The Heart of Lakeland,* Glasgow: Ernest Press, 1908.

Seatree, George, *Lakeland Memories,* Penrith: R.Scott, 1923.

Index

Published by Bookcase,

19 Castle Street, Carlisle, CA3 8SY,

01228 544560   www.bookscumbria.com

Printed and bound by CPI Antony Rowe, Eastbourne